**Contributing Editor**
Sara Connolly

**Editor in Chief**
Karen J. Goldfluss, M.S. Ed.

**Creative Director**
Sarah M. Fournier

**Cover Artist**
Sarah Kim

**Imaging**
James Edward Grace

**Publisher**
Mary D. Smith, M.S. Ed.

For correlations to the Common Core State Standards, see page 105 of this book or visit *http://www.teachercreated.com/standards/*.

**Teacher Created Resources**
12621 Western Avenue
Garden Grove, CA 92841
www.teachercreated.com
ISBN: 978-1-4206-8083-6

© 2017 Teacher Created Resources
Made in U.S.A.

# Table of Contents

# Introduction

The *Minutes to Mastery* series was designed to help students build confidence in their math abilities, and then bring that confidence into testing situations. As students develop fluency with math facts and operations, they improve their abilities to do different types of math problems comfortably and quickly.

Each of the 100 tests in the book has 10 questions in key math areas. Multiple opportunities are presented to solve the standards-based problems and develop speed and fluency. The pages present problems in a variety of ways using different terminology. For example, on a multiplication page, students might be asked to find the value of 36 tens or to multiply 36 times 10. Multiple terms are used to provide additional practice in decoding text for clues. Critical thinking and abstract reasoning play an important role in solving math problems, and practicing skills is imperative.

Keep in mind that timing can sometimes add to the stress of learning. If this is the experience for your math learner(s), focus less on timing in the beginning. As confidence builds, accuracy and speed will follow. Timing can be introduced later.

Following are steps to help you establish a timing system.

1. Allow students to complete a worksheet without officially timing it to get a sense of how long it will take them to complete it. Ideally, you want all ten questions per page to be answered.

2. Remind students to write their answers legibly.

3. Allow students to practice using the preferred amount of time before taking a timed test.

4. Have students take a few timed tests and see how it works. Adjust the time as needed.

5. Work to improve the number of correct answers within the given time. Remind students that it is important to be accurate—not just fast!

6. Encourage students to try to do their best each time, to review their results, and to spend time working on areas where they had difficulties.

The section at the bottom of each page can be used to record specific progress on that test, including the time the student started the test, finished the test, the total time taken, how many problems were completed, and how many problems were correct.

A tracking sheet is provided on page 4 of this book. Use the second column to record the number of problems students answered correctly, and the final column to record the score as a percent, the date the test was taken, initials, or anything else that helps you and your students to keep track of their progress.

With practice, all students can begin to challenge themselves to increase their speed while completing problems clearly and accurately.

# Tracking Sheet

Name _____

| Numbers | | |
|---|---|---|
| Test 1 | /10 | |
| Test 2 | /10 | |
| Test 3 | /10 | |
| Test 4 | /10 | |
| Test 5 | /10 | |
| Test 6 | /10 | |
| Test 7 | /10 | |
| Test 8 | /10 | |
| Test 9 | /10 | |
| Test 10 | /10 | |
| Test 11 | /10 | |
| Test 12 | /10 | |
| **Addition** | | |
| Test 13 | /10 | |
| Test 14 | /10 | |
| Test 15 | /10 | |
| Test 16 | /10 | |
| Test 17 | /10 | |
| Test 18 | /10 | |
| **Subtraction** | | |
| Test 19 | /10 | |
| Test 20 | /10 | |
| Test 21 | /10 | |
| Test 22 | /10 | |
| Test 23 | /10 | |
| Test 24 | /10 | |
| **Rounding and Estimation** | | |
| Test 25 | /10 | |
| Test 26 | /10 | |
| **Multiplication** | | |
| Test 27 | /10 | |
| Test 28 | /10 | |
| Test 29 | /10 | |
| Test 30 | /10 | |
| Test 31 | /10 | |
| Test 32 | /10 | |
| Test 33 | /10 | |
| Test 34 | /10 | |
| Test 35 | /10 | |

| Test 36 | /10 | |
|---|---|---|
| Test 37 | /10 | |
| Test 38 | /10 | |
| Test 39 | /10 | |
| **Division** | | |
| Test 40 | /10 | |
| Test 41 | /10 | |
| Test 42 | /10 | |
| Test 43 | /10 | |
| **Mixed Practice** | | |
| Test 44 | /10 | |
| Test 45 | /10 | |
| Test 46 | /10 | |
| Test 47 | /10 | |
| Test 48 | /10 | |
| **Fractions** | | |
| Test 49 | /10 | |
| Test 50 | /10 | |
| Test 51 | /10 | |
| Test 52 | /10 | |
| Test 53 | /10 | |
| **Decimals** | | |
| Test 54 | /10 | |
| Test 55 | /10 | |
| Test 56 | /10 | |
| Test 57 | /10 | |
| Test 58 | /10 | |
| Test 59 | /10 | |
| Test 60 | /10 | |
| Test 61 | /10 | |
| Test 62 | /10 | |
| Test 63 | /10 | |
| **Percentages** | | |
| Test 64 | /10 | |
| Test 65 | /10 | |
| Test 66 | /10 | |
| **Money** | | |
| Test 67 | /10 | |
| Test 68 | /10 | |
| Test 69 | /10 | |
| Test 70 | /10 | |

| Time | | |
|---|---|---|
| Test 71 | /10 | |
| Test 72 | /10 | |
| **Symmetry and Shapes** | | |
| Test 73 | /10 | |
| Test 74 | /10 | |
| Test 75 | /10 | |
| Test 76 | /10 | |
| **Angles and Lines** | | |
| Test 77 | /10 | |
| Test 78 | /10 | |
| Test 79 | /10 | |
| Test 80 | /10 | |
| **Shapes and 3D Objects** | | |
| Test 81 | /10 | |
| Test 82 | /10 | |
| Test 83 | /10 | |
| Test 84 | /10 | |
| Test 85 | /10 | |
| **Perimeter and Area** | | |
| Test 86 | /10 | |
| Test 87 | /10 | |
| **Position** | | |
| Test 88 | /10 | |
| Test 89 | /10 | |
| Test 90 | /10 | |
| **Probability** | | |
| Test 91 | /10 | |
| **Graphs and Data** | | |
| Test 92 | /10 | |
| Test 93 | /10 | |
| Test 94 | /10 | |
| **Problem Solving and Practice** | | |
| Test 95 | /10 | |
| Test 96 | /10 | |
| Test 97 | /10 | |
| Test 98 | /10 | |
| **Puzzles** | | |
| Test 99 | /10 | |
| Test 100 | /10 | |

Name _____     Date _____

## Write the number shown on each abacus.

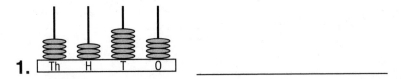

1. _____

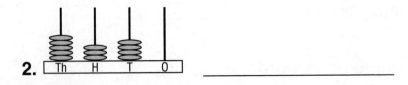

2. _____

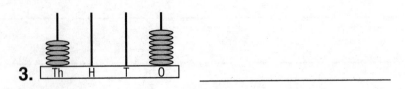

3. _____

## Write the numeral for each of the following.

4. seven thousand, three hundred seventy-two _____

5. five thousand, eleven _____

6. two thousand, one hundred one _____

7. two thousand, twenty-one _____

## Write each of the following numbers in words.

8. 1,275 _____

9. 2,041 _____

10. 7,009 _____

| Started: | Finished: | Total Time: | Completed: | Correct: |
|---|---|---|---|---|

Name _____ Date _____

## Write the numerals of the number words below.

**1.** two thousand, one hundred eighty-four _____

**2.** nine thousand, twenty-six _____

**3.** six thousand, three hundred sixty-one _____

## Write each of the following numbers in words.

**4.** 6,420 _____

**5.** 7,368 _____

**6.** 4,067 _____

**7.** 3,485 _____

## Write the following numbers in the place-value chart.

| Thousands | Hundreds | Tens | Ones |
|-----------|----------|------|------|
|           |          |      |      |
|           |          |      |      |
|           |          |      |      |

**8.** three thousand, one hundred eleven

**9.** two thousand, three hundred sixty-one

**10.** nine thousand, four hundred twenty-six

| Started: | Finished: | Total Time: | Completed: | Correct: |
|----------|-----------|-------------|------------|----------|

Name _____ Date _____

## Write the value of the underlined digit.

**1.** 3,<u>3</u>26 _____

**2.** 4,9<u>8</u>5 _____

**3.** 6,42<u>5</u> _____

**4.** <u>8</u>,865 _____

## Write *true* or *false* for each number statement.

**5.** 5,768 > 5,786 _____

**6.** 2,369 > 2,269 _____

**7.** 6,195 > 6,159 _____

## Use the digits 4, 8, 7, and 3 to answer the problems below.

**8.** Write the greatest possible 3-digit number without repeating any numbers.

_____

**9.** Write the least possible 4-digit number without repeating any numbers.

_____

**10.** Write the greatest possible 4-digit number without repeating any numbers.

_____

| Started: | Finished: | Total Time: | Completed: | Correct: |
|----------|-----------|-------------|------------|----------|

Name _____ Date _____

## Order the numbers below from least to greatest.

1.    2,065       2,111       2,011       2,089

     _____     _____     _____     _____

2.    3,033       3,303       3,330       3,003

     _____     _____     _____     _____

3.    2,649       3,841       8,916       1,824

     _____     _____     _____     _____

## Order the numbers below from greatest to least.

4.    7,860       6,980       6,650       8,970

     _____     _____     _____     _____

5.    1,111       1,101       1,010       1,011

     _____     _____     _____     _____

6.    5,403       5,609       5,905       5,302

     _____     _____     _____     _____

## Start at 1,359 and count forward by tens. Write the next five numbers in the pattern.

7. 1,359    _____    _____    _____    _____    _____

## Complete the following number patterns:

8.      8,002     8,004     8,006     _____     _____

9.      4,010     4,015     4,020     _____     _____

10.     3,100     3,090     3,080     _____     _____

| Started: | Finished: | Total Time: | Completed: | Correct: |
|---|---|---|---|---|

Name _____  Date _____

## Round the numbers below to the nearest thousand.

**1.** 2,222 _____

**2.** 8,456 _____

**3.** 6,885 _____

## Write the number that is 1,000 more than:

**4.** 4,249 _____

**5.** 8,456 _____

**6.** 3,346 _____

**7.** 5,052 _____

## Complete the following patterns.

| | | | | | |
|---|---|---|---|---|---|
| **8.** | 3,111 | 4,111 | 5,111 | _____ | _____ |
| **9.** | 6,789 | 5,789 | 4,789 | _____ | _____ |
| **10.** | 7,006 | 6,006 | 5,006 | _____ | _____ |

| Started: | Finished: | Total Time: | Completed: | Correct: |
|---|---|---|---|---|

Name _____  Date _____

## Write the numerals for the expanded numbers below.

**1.** 7,000 + 600 + 30 +1 _____

**2.** 1,000 + 900 + 4 _____

**3.** 3,000 + 300 + 30 + 3 _____

## Write the numbers and number word below in expanded form.

**4.** 5,528 _____

**5.** 2,999 _____

**6.** 6,709 _____

**7.** seven thousand, one hundred one _____

## Use the numeral expander to expand the following numbers.

**8.** 8,876

| | Th | | H | | T | | O |
|---|---|---|---|---|---|---|---|

**9.** 4,201

| | Th | | H | | T | | O |
|---|---|---|---|---|---|---|---|

**10.** 6,369

| | Th | | H | | T | | O |
|---|---|---|---|---|---|---|---|

| Started: | Finished: | Total Time: | Completed: | Correct: |
|---|---|---|---|---|

Name _____    Date _____

**If 8 people run in a sprint race,**

    **1.** in what position is the winner? _____

    **2.** what is the last position? _____

    **3.** what position is after 5th? _____

**If 100 people run in a marathon,**

    **4.** what position is after 11th? _____

    **5.** what position is after 20th? _____

    **6.** what positions are between 11th and 17th?

    _____

    **7.** what are the positions of the last five runners?

    _____

**Write the following as ordinal numbers.**

    **8.** third _____

    **9.** fifth _____

    **10.** fiftieth _____

| Started: | Finished: | Total Time: | Completed: | Correct: |
|----------|-----------|-------------|------------|----------|

Name _____ Date _____

## Find the factors of the following numbers.

**1.** 7 _____

**2.** 23 _____

**3.** 12 _____

## True or false?

**4.** 2 is a composite number. _____

**5.** 15 is a composite number. _____

**6.** 21 is a prime number. _____

**7.** 41 is a prime number. _____

## Label each of the following numbers as *prime* or *composite*.

**8.** 29 _____

**9.** 35 _____

**10.** 49 _____

| Started: | Finished: | Total Time: | Completed: | Correct: |
|---|---|---|---|---|

Name _____ Date _____

**Use doubles (multiplying by 2) to complete the following.**

**1.** double 10 = _____

double 20 = _____

4 × 10 = _____

**2.** double 15 = _____

double 30 = _____

4 × 15 = _____

**3.** double 21 = _____

double 42 = _____

4 × 21 = _____

**What number is halfway between the following numbers?**

**4.** 0 and 50 _____

**5.** 1,000 and 5,000 _____

**6.** 7,000 and 8,000 _____

**Find how many total legs are in the following groups of animals. Use the doubling method, if needed.**

**7.** How many total legs are on 16 tigers? _____

**8.** How many total legs are on 25 dogs? _____

**9.** How many total legs are on 50 elephants? _____

**10.** How many total legs are on 40 zebras? _____

| Started: | Finished: | Total Time: | Completed: | Correct: |
|----------|-----------|-------------|------------|----------|

# Numbers

Name _____  Date _____

## What number is

**1.** 5 greater than 1,015? _____

**2.** 10 greater than 3,694? _____

**3.** 5 less than 1,004? _____

**4.** 10 less than 3,762? _____

## Write *true* or *false* after the following number statements.

**5.** 863 < 683 _____

**6.** 3,469 > 3,496 _____

**7.** 2,751 > 2,571 _____

## Write the correct sign in the box to make each number statement true.

**8.** 325 ☐ 345

**9.** 1,349 ☐ 1,439

**10.** 9,256 ☐ 9,236

| Started: | Finished: | Total Time: | Completed: | Correct: |
|---|---|---|---|---|

Name _____  Date _____

## If you start at:

**1.** 100 and count by threes, what are the next five numbers you get?

_____

**2.** 100 and count backwards by fives, what are the next five numbers you get?

_____

**3.** 256 and count backwards by tens, what are the next five numbers you get?

_____

**4.** 3,416 and count by hundreds, what are the next five numbers you get?

_____

## What are the rules for these patterns?

**5.** 150, 200, 250, 300_____

**6.** 77, 70, 63, 56_____

**7.** 1,365; 1,265; 1,165; 1,065_____

## Fill in the missing numbers in each pattern.

**8.**   24          32          _____          48          _____

**9.**   597         589         _____     _____          565

**10.**  20          _____          60          _____          100

| Started: | Finished: | Total Time: | Completed: | Correct: |
|----------|-----------|-------------|------------|----------|

Name _____ Date _____

**Finish each pattern and write the rule.**

**1.** 3, 8, 13, 18, 23, _____, _____, _____, _____, _____, _____

The rule is:_____

**2.** 27, 25, 23, 21, 19, _____, _____, _____, _____, _____, _____

The rule is:_____

**3.** 25, 37, 49, 61, 73, _____, _____, _____, _____, _____, _____

The rule is:_____

**4.** 8, 15, 22, 29, 36, _____, _____, _____, _____, _____, _____

The rule is:_____

**5.** 49, 59, 69, 79, 89, _____, _____, _____, _____, _____, _____

The rule is:_____

**Look at each pattern. Write the rule.**

**6.**    75;       150;       300;       600;       1,200;       2,400

The rule is:_____

**7.**    10;       50;       250;       1,250;       6,250;       31,250

The rule is:_____

**8.**    7,290;       2,430;       810;       270;       90;       30

The rule is:_____

**9.**    12,800;       6,400;       3,200;       1,600;       800;       400

The rule is:_____

**10.**    13;       130;       1,300;       13,000;       130,000;       1,300,000

The rule is:_____

| Started: | Finished: | Total Time: | Completed: | Correct: |
|---|---|---|---|---|

Name _____        Date _____

## Solve the addition problems below.

| 1. | 41 | 2. | 23 | 3. | 19 | 4. | 65 |
|----|----|----|----|----|----|----|----|
|    | + 36 |  | + 71 |  | + 80 |  | + 30 |

## Solve the word problem below.

**5.** There were 16 horses on one farm and 23 on another. How many horses were there in all?

_____

## Find the missing numbers.

**6.** $15 + \_\_\_\_\_ = 53$

**7.** $\_\_\_\_\_ + 14 = 82$

## From the numbers below, find two numbers that total:

| 15 | 21 | 36 | 41 | 22 | 53 |
|----|----|----|----|----|----|

**8.** 43 _____

**9.** 56 _____

**10.** 89 _____

| Started: | Finished: | Total Time: | Completed: | Correct: |
|----------|-----------|-------------|------------|----------|

Name _____     Date _____

**Solve the addition problems below.**

| | | |
|---|---|---|
| **1.** 614<br>+ 323 | **2.** 785<br>+ 210 | **3.** 306<br>+ 290 |
| **4.** 120<br>+ 50 | **5.** 195<br>+ 203 | **6.** 727<br>+ 272 |

**Solve the word problem below.**

7. Omar had 321 cards in his collection. One year later, he had doubled his collection. How many cards did he have in the end?

_____

_____

**Estimate the sums by first rounding all numbers to the nearest ten. Then find the exact sums.**

|  | Estimate | Answer |
|---|---|---|
| **8.** 55 + 21 + 11 | _____ | _____ |
| **9.** 12 + 17 + 50 | _____ | _____ |
| **10.** 61 + 25 + 10 | _____ | _____ |

| Started: | Finished: | Total Time: | Completed: | Correct: |
|---|---|---|---|---|

Name _____ Date _____

## Solve the addition problems below.

1.    1,673
     + 3,026

2.    7,528
     + 1,360

3.    4,687
     + 3,212

4. Add 2,153 and 6,325. _____

5. Find the sum of 8,543 and 1,352. _____

6. Find the total of 4,326 and 1,350. _____

7. In one box, there were 2,467 paper clips. In a second box, there were 2,321 paper clips. How many paper clips were there all together?

_____

## Which numbers must be added to the following to make 9,999?

8. 6,305 _____

9. 2,456 _____

10. 8,721 _____

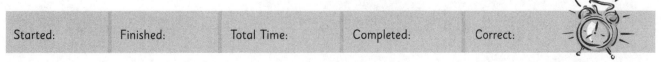

| Started: | Finished: | Total Time: | Completed: | Correct: |
|---|---|---|---|---|

Name _____ Date _____

## Solve the addition problems below.

1.    752
   + 109

2.    376
   + 430

3.    584
   + 244

4. Add 226 and 438. _____

5. Find the total of 743 and 157. _____

6. What is 256 plus 375? _____

7. If Riley has 129 pens and 457 pencils, how many writing tools does he have all together?

_____

**The school has the following boxes of supplies.**

| 295 erasers | 86 crayons | 173 pencils |

**Counted together, which of the items above gives a:**

8. total of 468? _____

9. total of 259? _____

10. total of 554? _____

| Started: | Finished: | Total Time: | Completed: | Correct: |

Name _____  Date _____

**Solve the addition problems below.**

| 1. | 2,062 | 2. | 3,250 | 3. | 3,333 | 4. | 1,905 |
|---|---|---|---|---|---|---|---|
|   | 1,524 |   | 1,905 |   | 2,136 |   | 2,063 |
|   | + 1,460 |   | + 2,153 |   | + 4,325 |   | + 4,012 |

5. On Monday, 1,236 newspapers were delivered. On Wednesday, 2,315 were delivered, and on Friday, 1,321 were delivered. How many newspapers were delivered all together?

_____

6. In the pet shop there were 496 fish in one tank, 327 in another, and 537 in a third. How many fish were there all together?

_____

7. The number of lemons picked on three different days were 1,379; 2,450; and 1,856. How many lemons were picked all together?

_____

**Find the sum. Then find what must be added to the sum to make 9,999.**

8. $3,050 + 2,690 = $ _____ + _____ $ = 9,999$

9. $5,631 + 2,506 = $ _____ + _____ $ = 9,999$

10. $3,625 + 1,375 = $ _____ + _____ $ = 9,999$

| Started: | Finished: | Total Time: | Completed: | Correct: |
|---|---|---|---|---|

     **Addition**

Name _____    Date _____

## Add the following.

**1.**    3,864
        1,972
    + 1,085

**2.**    3,847
        2,418
    + 1,385

**3.**    1,385
        1,268
    +1,101

## Find the total cost.

**4.** $1,321 + $4,653 + $3,201 = _____

**5.** $1,111 + $2,010 + $3,501 = _____

**6.** $999 + $2,995 + $2,050 = _____

**7.** $5,995 + $1,010 + $995 = _____

## Add the following

**8.**    123
       436
       129
   + 46

**9.** 1,025
      985
      103
   + 856

**10.**    2,050
       1,060
       4,250
    + 990

| Started: | Finished: | Total Time: | Completed: | Correct: |  |
|---|---|---|---|---|---|

Name _____ Date _____

**Solve the subtraction problems below.**

1.    56
   − 25

2.    69
   − 43

3.    73
   − 41

4.    89
   − 35

5. If a farmer had 66 sheep and sold 34, how many did she have left?

_____

6. There are 52 cards in a pack. If 11 were lost, how many cards are left?

_____

7. If there were 24 chocolates in the box and 13 were eaten, how many were left?

_____

**There are 58 bunches of flowers on a flower stand.**

8. If 37 bunches of flowers were sold, how many were left? _____

9. If 24 bunches of flowers were sold, how many were left? _____

10. If 46 bunches of flowers were sold, how many were left? _____

| Started: | Finished: | Total Time: | Completed: | Correct: |
| --- | --- | --- | --- | --- |

Subtraction

Name _____ Date _____

## Solve the subtraction problems below.

1.    81
  − 44

2.    86
  − 69

3.    72
  − 38

## Write *true* or *false* after each number statement.

**4.** 87 − 37 < 52 − 25 _____

**5.** 86 − 49 > 85 − 47 _____

**6.** 77 − 39 > 99 − 62 _____

## Find the missing number:

7.    95
  − ___
  70

## Some children are saving for scooters that cost $92. How much more does each child need to save if:

**8.** Arthur has $45? _____

**9.** Lily has $79? _____

**10.** Payal has $38? _____

| Started: | Finished: | Total Time: | Completed: | Correct: |
|---|---|---|---|---|

Name _____    Date _____

## Solve the subtraction problems below.

1.     856
    − 34

2.     698
    − 67

3.     273
    − 150

4.     778
    − 604

5. What is 18 less than 499? _____

6. How much greater is 189 than 56? _____

7. What do you get when you take away 45 from 165? _____

**If you have $256 in your bank account, how much do you have left if you:**

8. spend $123? _____

9. spend $46? _____

10. spend $215? _____

| Started: | Finished: | Total Time: | Completed: | Correct: |
|---|---|---|---|---|

Name _____ Date _____

**Solve the subtraction problems below.**

| 1. | 545<br>− 219 | 2. | 684<br>− 278 | 3. | 729<br>− 238 | 4. | 215<br>− 170 |

**Check these subtraction problems with addition:**

5.  142
    − 61
    [ ]   →   [ ]
              + 61
              [ ]

6.  475
    − 229
    [ ]   →   [ ]
              + 229
              [ ]

7.  800
    − 321
    [ ]   →   [ ]
              + 321
              [ ]

**At the state fair, there were 852 cows, 735 sheep, and 463 goats. How many more:**

**8.** cows than sheep are there? _____

**9.** sheep than goats are there? _____

**10.** cows than goats are there? _____

| Started: | Finished: | Total Time: | Completed: | Correct: |

Name _____ Date _____

## Solve the subtraction problems below.

| 1. | 3,834 | 2. | 3,945 | 3. | 6,750 | 4. | 9,999 |
|----|-------|----|-------|----|-------|----|-------|
|    | − 2,312 |  | − 2,810 |  | − 4,510 |  | − 7,653 |

## Find the missing numbers.

**5.**  4 , 6  2  7

     − 2 ,___ 1 ___
_____

     ___ , 3 ___ 1

**6.**  7 , 4  9  3

     − 6 ,___ 4 ___
_____

     ___ , 2 ___ 0

**7.**  5 ,___ 7 ___

     − 2 , 4  1  5
_____

     ___ , 3 ___ 1

## Using the digits 4, 6, 3, and 1, write:

**8.** the greatest possible 4-digit number. _____

**9.** the least possible 4-digit number. _____

**10.** Find the difference between the two numbers that you wrote.

_____

| Started: | Finished: | Total Time: | Completed: | Correct: |
|----------|-----------|-------------|------------|----------|

Name _____ Date _____

## Solve the subtraction problems below.

1. 4,365
 − 1,285

2. 5,472
 − 4,319

3. 3,000
 − 1,451

4. 8,754
 − 5,276

5. Find the difference between 4,637 and 1,952. _____

6. Subtract 4,259 from 6,463. _____

7. What is 9,221 minus 4,635? _____

## Find the difference between 5,000 and:

8. 2,451 _____

9. 1,985 _____

10. 3,625 _____

| Started: | Finished: | Total Time: | Completed: | Correct: |
| --- | --- | --- | --- | --- |

Name _____ Date _____

## Do you round:

**1.** 732 to 700 or 800? _____

**2.** 1,350 to 1,000 or 2,000? _____

**3.** 7,795 to 7,000 or 8,000? _____

## Round:

**4.** 153 to the nearest 10. _____

**5.** 278 to the nearest 10. _____

**6.** 5,610 to the nearest 100. _____

**7.** 8,374 to the nearest 100. _____

**Circle the number (or numbers) in each group that, if rounded to the nearest thousand, would be rounded to 5,000.**

**8.** 4,965          4,225          4,835

**9.** 4,775          4,395          4,105

**10.** 4,665          4,095          4,595

| Started: | Finished: | Total Time: | Completed: | Correct: |
|---|---|---|---|---|

Name _____ Date _____

**Round each number to the nearest ten and then estimate the answer.**

**1.** 27 + 51= _____

**2.** 412 + 93 = _____

**3.** 144 − 38 = _____

**Round each number to the nearest ten and circle the best estimate for the sum or difference.**

**4.** 49 + 98 + 201     _____    350   370   390

**5.** 100 − 34 − 14 − 9     _____    40    50    60

**6.** 500 − 182 − 59 − 62   _____    180   200   220

**7.** 132 + 132 + 132 + 132  _____    480   500   520

**Estimate each answer by first rounding each number to the nearest ten. Then find the actual answer. Finally, find the difference between the estimate and the actual answer.**

| | Question | Estimate | Actual | Difference |
|---|---|---|---|---|
| **8.** | 129 + 32 | | | |
| **9.** | 319 + 56 | | | |
| **10.** | 578 − 304 | | | |

Name _____ Date _____

**Complete the number sentences to find the total number of dots.**

1. 3 groups of 4 dots = _____ dots

2. 4 groups of _____ dots = _____ dots

3. 3 groups of _____ dots = _____ dots

**Use doubles to calculate the following.**

4. double 12 = 24

    double 24 = _____

    4 × 12 = _____

5. double 16 = _____

    double _____ = _____

    4 × 16 = _____

6. double 28 = _____

    double _____ = _____

    4 × 28 = _____

7. double 33 = _____

    double _____ = _____

    4 × 33 = _____

**To make multiplication of multi-digit numbers easier, split two-digit numbers into tens and ones. Multiply each value separately and then add the results together.**

8. 14 × 8

    = (10 × 8) + (4 × 8)

    = _____ + _____

    = _____

9. 13 × 6

    = (10 × 6) + (3 × 6)

    = _____ + _____

    = _____

10. 18 × 5

    = (10 × 5) + (8 × 5)

    = _____ + _____

    = _____

| Started: | Finished: | Total Time: | Completed: | Correct: |
|---|---|---|---|---|

Name _____ Date _____

**Divide each number in half and repeat for as long as the numbers are whole (i.e., no fractions or decimals).**

**1.** 16, _____

**2.** 160, _____

**3.** 256, _____

**Double the number, and keep doubling five times for each number.**

**4.** 9, _____

**5.** 5, _____

**6.** 100, _____

**Find the mistake in each problem's answer and correct it.**

```
7.    459          8.    374
    + 107              − 135
    ─────              ─────
      466                249
```

**Are the following number sentences *true* or *false*?**

**9.** 22 + 22 + 22 = 3 × 22 _____

**10.** 21 − 14 = 14 − 21 _____

| Started: | Finished: | Total Time: | Completed: | Correct: |
|----------|-----------|-------------|------------|----------|

Name _____ Date _____

## Multiply the following:

**1.** 3 × 8 = _____

**2.** 11 × 2 = _____

**3.** 9 × 4 = _____

## Find the product of:

**4.** 10 and 2 _____

**5.** 7 and 8 _____

## Complete the problems below.

**6.** Write the first 10 multiples of 4

_____

**7.** There were 10 cars and 12 bicycles in a small parking lot. How many total wheels were there?

_____

## Find the number of legs on:

**8.** 9 spiders. _____

**9.** 8 cows. _____

**10.** 12 chickens. _____

| Started: | Finished: | Total Time: | Completed: | Correct: |
|----------|-----------|-------------|------------|----------|

Name _____ Date _____

## Multiply the following:

**1.** $12 \times 5 =$ _____

**2.** $3 \times 10 =$ _____

**3.** $5 \times 0 =$ _____

**4.** Find the product of 9 and 5. _____

**5.** What is 11 times 10? _____

## True or false?

**6.** $2 \times 5 = 1 \times 10$ _____

**7.** $8 \times 5 = 4 \times 10$ _____

## Complete the following multiplication wheels.

**8.**

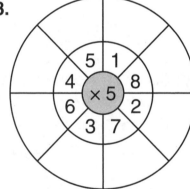

**9.**

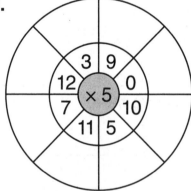

**10.**

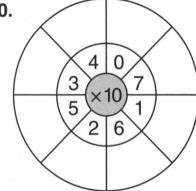

| Started: | Finished: | Total Time: | Completed: | Correct: |
|----------|-----------|-------------|------------|----------|

Name _____ Date _____

## Multiply the following:

**1.** $12 \times 6 =$ _____

**2.** $10 \times 3 =$ _____

**3.** $6 \times 7 =$ _____

## Find the missing numbers.

**4.** $3 \times$ _____ $= 12 =$ _____ $\times 6$

**5.** $6 \times$ _____ $=$ _____ $= 4 \times 9$

**6.** $10 \times$ _____ $= 30 =$ _____ $\times 5$

## Solve the following word problem.

**7.** At the bake sale, Jenna bought 5 dozen cupcakes for $6 per dozen. How much did Jenna pay for cupcakes?

_____

## Write an equation to show each of the following, and then solve each one.

**8.** corners on 7 triangles _____

**9.** eyes on 6 pandas _____

**10.** wheels on 11 tricycles _____

| Started: | Finished: | Total Time: | Completed: | Correct: |
|---|---|---|---|---|

Name _____ Date _____

## Multiply the following:

**1.** $7 \times 5 =$ _____

**2.** $6 \times 8 =$ _____

**3.** $8 \times 9 =$ _____

## Write *true* or *false* after each equation.

**4.** $7 \times 4 = 3 \times 8$ _____

**5.** $0 \times 9 = 0 \times 7$ _____

**6.** $7 \times 8 = 8 \times 9$ _____

## Count by eights starting at 50. Write down the next ten numbers.

**7.** 50, _____, _____, _____, _____, _____, _____, _____,

_____, _____, _____

## Complete the following multiplication wheels.

**8.**

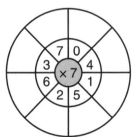

**9.**

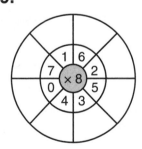

**10.**

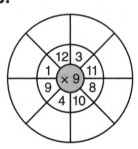

| Started: | Finished: | Total Time: | Completed: | Correct: |
|---|---|---|---|---|

# Multiplication

Name _____ Date _____

## Multiply the following:

**1.**  10
   x  8

**2.**  9
   x 7

**3.**  8
   x 5

**4.** How much do 6 movie tickets cost at $8 each? _____

**5.** How much do 7 chocolate bars cost at $2 each? _____

## Find the missing numbers.

**6.** $10 \times 3 =$ _____ $= 6 \times$ _____

**7.** $9 \times$ _____ $=$ _____ $= 3 \times 6$

## Complete the multiplication charts.

**8.**

| x | 6 | 7 | 8 | 9 |
|---|---|---|---|---|
| 8 |   |   |   |   |

**9.**

| x | 5 | 6 | 7 | 8 |
|---|---|---|---|---|
| 9 |   |   |   |   |

**10.**

| x | 8 | 9 | 10 | 11 |
|---|---|---|---|---|
| 5 |   |   |   |   |

| Started: | Finished: | Total Time: | Completed: | Correct: |
|---|---|---|---|---|

                                *Multiplication*

Name _____ Date _____

## Find the following square numbers:

**1.** 2 squared = _____

**2.** 7 squared = _____

**3.** 9 × 9 = _____

## Find the following triangular numbers:

**4.** 1 + 2 + 3 + 4 + 5 = _____

**5.** 1 + 2 + 3 + 4 + 5 + 6 = _____

**6.** ⬚ = _____

**7.** ⬚ = _____

## Draw the following numbers using dots.

**8.** 3 squared            **9.** 4 squared            **10.** 5 squared

| Started: | Finished: | Total Time: | Completed: | Correct: |
|---|---|---|---|---|

Name _____ Date _____

## True or false?

**1.** 36 is a multiple of 9. _____

**2.** 14 is a multiple of 6. _____

**3.** 90 is a multiple of 10. _____

## Complete the following:

**4.** 12 is a multiple of _____ and _____.

**5.** 35 is a multiple of _____ and _____.

**6.** 32 is a multiple of _____ and _____.

**7.** Which of the numbers 14, 7, or 15 is a multiple of 5? _____

## Which of the numbers 10, 12, 18, or 21 are multiples of:

**8.** 2? _____

**9.** 3? _____

**10.** 7? _____

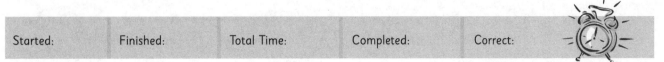

| Started: | Finished: | Total Time: | Completed: | Correct: |
|---|---|---|---|---|

Name _____ Date _____

## Write one pair of factors for each number

**1.** 5: _____, _____

**2.** 11: _____, _____

**3.** 23: _____, _____

## True or false?

**4.** 3 is a factor of 10. _____

**5.** 6 is a factor of 42. _____

## List all the factors of the following:

**6.** 15: _____, _____, _____, _____

**7.** 24: _____, _____, _____, _____, _____, _____, _____, _____

## List all the factors of 36 and 18.

**8.** 36: _____

**9.** 18: _____

**10.** Circle the factors above that 36 and 18 have in common.

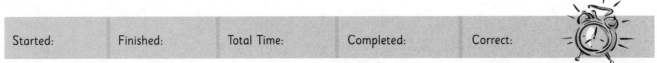

| Started: | Finished: | Total Time: | Completed: | Correct: |
|----------|-----------|-------------|------------|----------|

Name _____  Date _____

**To make multiplication of multi-digit numbers easier, split two-digit numbers into tens and ones. Multiply each value separately and then add the results together.**

**1.** $16 \times 5$

$= (10 \times 5) + (6 \times 5)$

$=$ _____ + _____

$=$ _____

**2.** $19 \times 6$

$= (10 \times 6) + (9 \times 6)$

$=$ _____ + _____

$=$ _____

**3.** $14 \times 8$

$= (10 \times 8) + ($ _____ $\times$ _____ $)$

$=$ _____ + _____

$=$ _____

**Multiplying with multiples of ten is the same as single digit multiplication, except a zero is added to the answer (e.g., $5 \times 5 = 25$ and $5 \times 50 = 250$). Complete each of the following using this strategy.**

**4.**  40
    x  5

**5.**  60
    x  8

**6.**  80
    x  4

**Multiplying with multiples of one hundred is the same as single digit multiplication, except two zeros are added to the answer (e.g., $5 \times 5 = 25$ and $5 \times 500 = 2,500$). Complete each of the following using this strategy.**

**7.**  400
    x  8

**8.**  500
    x  6

**9.**  900
    x  3

**10.**  700
    x  4

| Started: | Finished: | Total Time: | Completed: | Correct: |
|----------|-----------|-------------|------------|----------|

Name _____ Date _____

## Find the value of:

**1.** 6 tens = _____

**2.** 14 tens = _____

**3.** 56 tens = _____

## Multiply the following:

**4.** $36 \times 10 =$ _____

**5.** $42 \times 10 =$ _____

**6.** $33 \times 10 =$ _____

**7.** There are 81 rows of seats with 10 seats per row inside Teddy's Theater. How many total seats are in the theater?

_____

## Multiply the following by first breaking down the greater number into a single-digit number times 10.

**8.** $5 \times 60$

    $= 5 \times 6 \times 10$

    $=$ _____

**9.** $7 \times 30$

    $= 7 \times 3 \times 10$

    $=$ _____

**10.** $5 \times 90$

    $= 5 \times 9 \times 10$

    $=$ _____

| Started: | Finished: | Total Time: | Completed: | Correct: |
|---|---|---|---|---|

Name _____ Date _____

## Complete the multiplication pattern.

**1.** $2 \times 6 =$ _____      **2.** $5 \times 7 =$ _____

$20 \times 6 =$ _____      $50 \times 7 =$ _____

$200 \times 6 =$ _____      $500 \times 7 =$ _____

## Multiply the following:

**3.**    32       **4.**    53       **5.**    41       **6.**    65
    x 4         x 6         x 5         x 6

## Solve the following word problem.

**7.** Find the total number of bananas if there are 26 in each of 8 boxes.

_____

**To make multiplication of multi-digit numbers easier, split two-digit numbers into tens and ones. Multiply each value separately and then add the results together.**

**8.** $2 \times 43$

$= (2 \times 40) + (2 \times 3)$

$=$ _____ $+$ _____

$=$ _____

**9.** $6 \times 16$

$= (6 \times$ _____ $) + (6 \times$ _____ $)$

$=$ _____ $+$ _____

$=$ _____

**10.** $4 \times 53$

$= (4 \times$ _____ $) + (4 \times$ _____ $)$

$=$ _____ $+$ _____

$=$ _____

| Started: | Finished: | Total Time: | Completed: | Correct: |
|---|---|---|---|---|

Name _____   Date _____

**Use the multiplication equations to complete the division problems.**

**1.** $9 \times 8 = 72$          **2.** $6 \times 7 = 42$          **3.** $12 \times 4 = 48$

$9\overline{)72}$                      $6\overline{)42}$                      $4\overline{)48}$

$8\overline{)72}$                      $7\overline{)42}$                      $12\overline{)48}$

**Divide the following:**

**4.** $54 \div 6 =$ _____

**5.** $68 \div 2 =$ _____

**6.** $96 \div 8 =$ _____

**7.** How many groups of 6 are there in 36? _____

**How many baskets are needed for each situation?**

**8.** 70 strawberries, 10 in each basket _____

**9.** 40 apples, 8 in each basket _____

**10.** 9 puppies, 3 in each basket _____

| Started: | Finished: | Total Time: | Completed: | Correct: |
|---|---|---|---|---|

Name _____ Date _____

| x | 0 | 1 | 2 | 3 | 4 | 5 | 6 | 7 | 8 | 9 | 10 |
|---|---|---|---|---|---|---|---|---|---|---|----|
| 0 | 0 | 0 | 0 | 0 | 0 | 0 | 0 | 0 | 0 | 0 | 0 |
| 1 | 0 | 1 | 2 | 3 | 4 | 5 | 6 | 7 | 8 | 9 | 10 |
| 2 | 0 | 2 | 4 | 6 | 8 | 10 | 12 | 14 | 16 | 18 | 20 |
| 3 | 0 | 3 | 6 | 9 | 12 | 15 | 18 | 21 | 24 | 27 | 30 |
| 4 | 0 | 4 | 8 | 12 | 16 | 20 | 24 | 28 | 32 | 36 | 40 |
| 5 | 0 | 5 | 10 | 15 | 20 | 25 | 30 | 35 | 40 | 45 | 50 |
| 6 | 0 | 6 | 12 | 18 | 24 | 30 | 36 | 42 | 48 | 54 | 60 |
| 7 | 0 | 7 | 14 | 21 | 28 | 35 | 42 | 49 | 56 | 63 | 70 |
| 8 | 0 | 8 | 16 | 24 | 32 | 40 | 48 | 56 | 64 | 72 | 80 |
| 9 | 0 | 9 | 18 | 27 | 36 | 45 | 54 | 63 | 72 | 81 | 90 |
| 10 | 0 | 10 | 20 | 30 | 40 | 50 | 60 | 70 | 80 | 90 | 100 |

**Use the multiplication grid to answer the following:**

**1.** $24 \div 6 =$ _____    **2.** $50 \div 5 =$ _____    **3.** $64 \div 8 =$ _____

**Use the multiplication grid to fill in the spaces.**

**4.** $27 \div$ _____ $= 9$          **5.** _____ $\div 5 = 5$

**6.** $81 \div$ _____ $= 9$          **7.** _____ $\div 3 = 8$

**Use the multiplication grid to complete the following.**

**8.** $7\overline{)56}$          **9.** $4\overline{)32}$          **10.** $8\overline{)48}$

| Started: | Finished: | Total Time: | Completed: | Correct: |
|----------|-----------|-------------|------------|----------|

Name _____     Date _____

## Find the missing numbers:

**1.** _____ × 9 = 27

**2.** 4 × _____ = 32

**3.** 3 × _____ = 30

**4.** 28 ÷ _____ = 7

**5.** 20 ÷ _____ = 10

**6.** 54 ÷ _____ = 6

## Solve the following word problem.

**7.** Janet is using a box of 49 beads to make necklaces. If Janet uses 7 beads for each necklace, how many necklaces can she make?

_____

## Solve each problem. Write the answer and the remainder.

**8.** There are 32 bottles in 6 equal rows. How many bottles are in each row and how many are left over?

_____

**9.** There are 63 cows in herds of 10. How many complete herds are there and how many cows are left over?

_____

**10.** There are 96 marbles in 9 equal groups. How many marbles are in each group and how many are left over?

_____

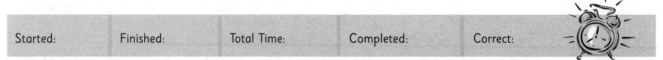

| Started: | Finished: | Total Time: | Completed: | Correct: |
|----------|-----------|-------------|------------|----------|

Name _____  Date _____

## Use the first equation to complete the second one and find the remainder.

**1.** $(5 \times 4) + 3 = 23$        **2.** $(8 \times 3) + 2 = 26$        **3.** $(6 \times 7) + 5 = 47$

$23 \div 4 =$ _____           $26 \div 3 =$ _____           $47 \div 7 =$ _____

## Divide the following:

**4.** $36 \div 2 =$ _____

**5.** $9\overline{)100} =$ _____

**6.** $6\overline{)39} =$ _____

## Solve the following word problem.

**7.** Alyssa's mom baked 29 cookies for Alyssa and 5 of her friends to eat. If each person will eat the same number of cookies, how many will each person eat? How many will be left over?

_____

## Complete each path.

**8.** $70 \div 7 \rightarrow$ _____ $\times 3 \rightarrow$ _____ $\div 5 \rightarrow$ _____ $\times 3 \rightarrow$ _____

**9.** $64 \div 8 \rightarrow$ _____ $\times 2 \rightarrow$ _____ $\div 4 \rightarrow$ _____ $\times 10 \rightarrow$ _____

**10.** $45 \div 9 \rightarrow$ _____ $\times 10 \rightarrow$ _____ $\times 2 \rightarrow$ _____ $\div 10 \rightarrow$ _____

| Started: | Finished: | Total Time: | Completed: | Correct: |
|----------|-----------|-------------|------------|----------|

Name _____ Date _____

## Complete the following.

**1.** $2 \times 3 \times 4 =$ _____

**2.** $5 \times 8 \times 6 =$ _____

## Complete each number sentence with >, <, or = to make it true.

**3.** $36 \div 6$ ☐ $18 \div 3$

**4.** $42 \div 6$ ☐ $3 \times 4$

**5.** $14 - 8$ ☐ $8 \times 0$

## Solve the word problems below.

**6.** There are 4 hens in the pen, and each hen laid 6 eggs this week. How many eggs are there all together?

_____

**7.** I bought 2 loaves of bread for $2.50 each, some cheese for $3.50, and an apple for 50¢. How much did I pay all together?

_____

## Fill in the missing numbers to complete the equations.

**8.** $80 -$ _____ $= 34$

**9.** _____ $\times 2 \times 4 = 56$

**10.** $29 +$ _____ $+ 11 = 60$

| Started: | Finished: | Total Time: | Completed: | Correct: |
|----------|-----------|-------------|------------|----------|

Name _____ Date _____

**Find the missing numbers.**

**1.** _____ × 9 = 63        **2.** 4 × _____ = 8

**Divide the following:**

**3.** 5)‾85̅        **4.** 3)‾81̅        **5.** 6)‾78̅

**Complete the word problems below.**

**6.** Helen had 8 chickens in each of 6 pens. How many chickens were there all together?

_____

**7.** Albert divided 98 nails into 7 boxes. How many nails were there in each box?

_____

**Write one multiplication fact and one division fact for each set of numbers in the triangles.**

**8.** /35\ /5  7\        _____

_____

**9.** /30\ /3  10\        _____

_____

**10.** /4\ /1  4\        _____

_____

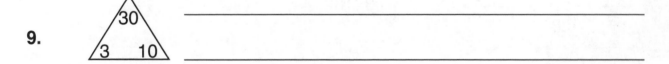

| Started: | Finished: | Total Time: | Completed: | Correct: |
|----------|-----------|-------------|------------|----------|

Name _____ Date _____

**Check the subtraction fact with addition, and write *true* or *false*.**

**1.** 43 – 26 = 17 _____

**2.** 85 – 27 = 58 _____

**3.** 90 – 26 = 74 _____

**Check the addition fact with subtraction, and write *true* or *false*.**

**4.** 49 + 21 = 60 _____

**5.** 36 + 16 = 52 _____

**6.** 84 + 27 = 101 _____

**Solve the following word problem.**

**7.** Molly had 23 bracelets. After opening her birthday gifts, Molly now has 37 bracelets. Write the equation and solve it to show how many bracelets Molly got for her birthday.

_____

**Find the mistakes in each of the following problems. Write the correct answers.**

**8.**   49
      x 2
     ――――
       88

**9.**      64
     3 )‾1‾3‾2‾

**10.**     12
      9 )‾1‾2‾6‾

| Started: | Finished: | Total Time: | Completed: | Correct: |  |

Name _____ Date _____

**Use the number line to solve the addition and subtraction equations by "jumping up" and "jumping down" the number line.**

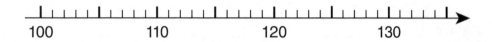

100      110      120      130

**1.** $109 + 19 =$ _____

**2.** $102 + 26 =$ _____

**3.** $130 - 16 =$ _____

**4.** $125 - 18 =$ _____

**5.** $133 - 19 =$ _____

**Use the number line to complete the multiplication and division equations.**

0      10      20      30

**6.** $2 \times 15 =$ _____

**7.** $24 \div 6 =$ _____

**8.** $5 \times 4 =$ _____

**9.** $35 \div 7 =$ _____

**10.** $25 \div 5 =$ _____

| Started: | Finished: | Total Time: | Completed: | Correct: |
|---|---|---|---|---|

Name _____  Date _____

**Continue each pattern by following the rule.**

   **1.** Add 5: 20, _____, _____, _____

   **2.** Multiply by 2: 5, _____, _____, _____

   **3.** Subtract 9: 100, _____, _____, _____

**Write the next number in each pattern.**

   **4.** 1, 5, 25, _____

   **5.** 10, 21, 32, _____

   **6.** 4, 8, 16, _____

   **7.** 103, 100, 97, _____

**These patterns have 2 steps in each rule. Both steps must be done to get to the next number. Write the next three terms in each pattern.**

   **8.** Rule: $\times 3 + 1$

      1, 4, _____, _____, _____

   **9.** Rule: $\times 10 - 5$

      1, 5, _____, _____, _____

  **10.** Rule: $- 1 + 5$

      10, 14, _____, _____, _____

| Started: | Finished: | Total Time: | Completed: | Correct: |
|---|---|---|---|---|

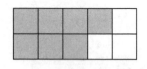

Name _____ Date _____

## What fraction of each shape is shaded?

**1.**

_____

**2.**
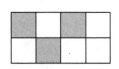

_____

**3.**

_____

## Write *true* or *false* for each statement.

**4.** $\frac{9}{10} = 1$ _____

**5.** $1 = \frac{4}{4}$ _____

## Write each of the following fractions in words.

**6.** $\frac{1}{4}$ _____

**7.** $\frac{2}{5}$ _____

## Name the fraction of each group that is shaded.

**8.** ▲▲▲△△ _____

**9.** ★★★★☆☆☆☆☆ _____

**10.** ●●●●○○○○ _____

| Started: | Finished: | Total Time: | Completed: | Correct: |
|----------|-----------|-------------|------------|----------|

Name _____  Date _____

## Order the fractions from least to greatest.

**1.** $\frac{2}{8}, \frac{5}{8}, \frac{1}{8}, \frac{7}{8}$ _____

**2.** $\frac{4}{5}, \frac{2}{5}, \frac{3}{5}, \frac{1}{5}$ _____

**3.** $\frac{1}{10}, \frac{3}{10}, \frac{4}{10}, \frac{2}{10}$ _____

## Order the fractions from greatest to least.

**4.** $\frac{9}{10}, \frac{6}{10}, \frac{4}{10}, \frac{8}{10}$ _____

**5.** $\frac{3}{4}, \frac{2}{4}, \frac{1}{4}, \frac{4}{4}$ _____

**6.** $\frac{1}{2}, \frac{1}{10}, \frac{1}{5}, \frac{4}{10}$ _____

## Shade part of the group to match the given fraction.

**7.** $\frac{7}{10}$ of the stars

☆ ☆ ☆ ☆ ☆ ☆ ☆ ☆ ☆ ☆

## Shade the fraction of each shape.

**8.** $\frac{1}{2}$

**9.** $\frac{1}{4}$

**10.** $\frac{5}{8}$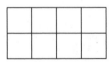

| Started: | Finished: | Total Time: | Completed: | Correct: |
|---|---|---|---|---|

Name _____  Date _____

## Circle the greater fraction.

**1.**    $\frac{1}{5}$    or    $\frac{1}{4}$          **2.**    $\frac{1}{2}$    or    $\frac{3}{4}$

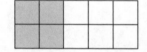    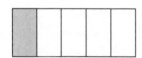            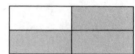

**3.**    $\frac{4}{10}$    or    $\frac{3}{5}$

## Write *true* or *false* for each statement.

**4.** $1 = \frac{5}{5}$ _____

**5.** $1 = \frac{9}{10}$ _____

**6.** $1 = \frac{4}{4}$ _____

## Order the fractions from greatest to least.

**7.** $\frac{3}{8}, \frac{5}{8}, \frac{4}{8}, \frac{1}{8}$ _____

**8.** $\frac{2}{10}, \frac{6}{10}, \frac{3}{10}, \frac{9}{10}$ _____

## Order the numbers from least to greatest.

**9.** $\frac{1}{2}, \frac{3}{4}, 1, \frac{1}{4}$ _____

**10.** $\frac{7}{8}, 1, \frac{5}{8}, \frac{6}{8}$ _____

| Started: | Finished: | Total Time: | Completed: | Correct: |
|----------|-----------|-------------|------------|----------|

Name _____ Date _____

**Shade and write an equivalent fraction for the one given.**

**1.** $\frac{1}{2}$ or $\frac{}{4}$

**2.** $\frac{1}{2}$ or $\frac{}{10}$

**3.** $\frac{3}{4}$ or $\frac{}{8}$

**True or false?**

**4.** $\frac{1}{2} = \frac{3}{4}$ _____

**5.** $\frac{6}{10} = \frac{3}{5}$ _____

**Write the missing number in the equivalent fraction for the following fractions.**

**6.** $\frac{4}{10} = \frac{}{5}$

**7.** $\frac{6}{8} = \frac{}{4}$

**Use the number line to help find the equivalent fractions. Give the number of:**

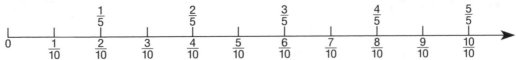

**8.** tenths in five-fifths _____

**9.** tenths in one-fifth _____

**10.** fifths in four-tenths _____

| Started: | Finished: | Total Time: | Completed: | Correct: |
| --- | --- | --- | --- | --- |

Name _____  Date _____

## What fraction is shaded in the following diagrams?

**1.** _____

**2.** _____

**3.** _____

## Complete the number lines.

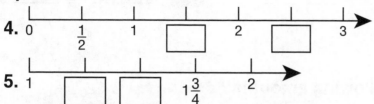

**4.** 0    $\frac{1}{2}$    1    ☐    2    ☐    3

**5.** 1    ☐    ☐    $1\frac{3}{4}$    2

## Circle the greater mixed number in the pair below.

**6.** $1\frac{2}{5}$    $1\frac{3}{5}$

## Circle the lesser mixed number in the pair below.

**7.** $3\frac{1}{4}$    $2\frac{3}{4}$

## Shade the shapes to show the mixed numbers.

**8.** $1\frac{3}{5}$

**9.** $1\frac{5}{8}$

**10.** $1\frac{6}{8}$

| Started: | Finished: | Total Time: | Completed: | Correct: |
|---|---|---|---|---|

Name _____ Date _____

## What fraction of each hundreds square is shaded?

1.

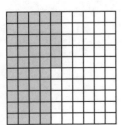

_____

2.

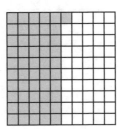

_____

3.

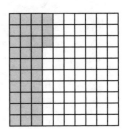

_____

## How many cents are in the following amounts?

**4.** $2.90 _____

**5.** $1.75 _____

**6.** $5.05 _____

## Write each of the following as a decimal.

**7.** five hundredths _____

**8.** sixty-two hundredths _____

**9.** forty hundredths _____

**10.** nineteen hundredths _____

| Started: | Finished: | Total Time: | Completed: | Correct: |
|---|---|---|---|---|

Name _____    Date _____

## Use digits to write the following decimals.

**1.** six-tenths _____

**2.** seven-tenths _____

## Draw lines to match each fraction with the correct decimal.

**3.**    $1\frac{1}{10}$                    0.2

**4.**    $\frac{5}{10}$                    0.3

**5.**    $\frac{2}{10}$                    1

**6.**    $\frac{10}{10}$                    1.1

**7.**    $1\frac{7}{10}$                    1.7

**8.**    $\frac{3}{10}$                    0.5

## Charlie was practicing shooting free throws in basketball practice. Out of ten free-throw attempts, Charlie made seven free throws.

**9.** Write the decimal that shows the portion of free throws that Charlie made.

_____

**10.** Write the decimal that shows the portion of free throws that Charlie missed.

_____

| Started: | Finished: | Total Time: | Completed: | Correct: |
|----------|-----------|-------------|------------|----------|

Name _____    Date _____

## Write the decimal that is shaded on each hundreds square.

**1.**                           **2.**                           **3.**

          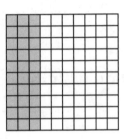          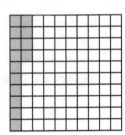

_____        _____        _____

## Give the value of the 5 in each of the following numbers.

**4.** 1.56 _____

**5.** 3.05 _____

**6.** 56.20 _____

**7.** 15.92 _____

## Write each of the following decimals in words.

**8.** 0.46 _____

**9.** 0.05 _____

**10.** 0.30 _____

| Started: | Finished: | Total Time: | Completed: | Correct: |
|---|---|---|---|---|

# Decimals

Name _____ Date _____

**Circle the greatest decimal in the following groups.**

   **1.**    0.75      0.57      0.67

   **2.**    0.39      0.93      0.65

**Circle the least decimal in the following groups.**

   **3.**    0.40      0.51      0.63

   **4.**    0.29      0.36      0.17

**Write each number in decimal form.**

   **5.** 5 tenths and 7 hundredths _____

   **6.** 4 tenths and 2 hundredths _____

**Give the value of the underlined digit.**

   **7.** 0.4̲3 _____

**Place each of the following numbers in the chart.**

| H | T | O | . | Tths | Hths |
|---|---|---|---|------|------|
| | | | | | |
| | | | | | |
| | | | | | |

**8.** 12.40

**9.** 205.66

**10.** 310.95

| Started: | Finished: | Total Time: | Completed: | Correct: |
|----------|-----------|-------------|------------|----------|

Name _____ Date _____

## Write the next decimal in each of the patterns.

**1.** 0.11, 0.12, _____

**2.** 0.77, 0.78, _____

**3.** 0.03, 0.04, _____

## Round each decimal to the nearest whole number.

**4.** 2.34 _____

**5.** 6.75 _____

## Round each decimal to the nearest tenth.

**6.** 4.21 _____

**7.** 4.58 _____

## Order each set of decimals from least to greatest.

**8.** 0.15, 0.05, 0.50, 0.45 _____

**9.** 1.21, 1.28, 1.27, 1.23 _____

**10.** 1.46, 2.38, 1.79, 3.66 _____

| Started: | Finished: | Total Time: | Completed: | Correct: |

Name _____     Date _____

**Write each of the following in decimal form.**

   **1.** 1 and 27 hundredths _____

   **2.** 5 and 6 hundredths _____

   **3.** 1 and 19 hundredths _____

**Round each of the following decimals to the nearest whole number.**

   **4.** 1.09 _____

   **5.** 2.72 _____

   **6.** 3.45 _____

**Order this set of decimals from least to greatest.**

   **7.** 19.63, 20.58, 17.62, 14.32

   _____

**Circle the correct decimal that matches the mixed number.**

   **8.** $1\frac{16}{100}$        1.91            1.6            1.16

   **9.** $1\frac{50}{100}$        1.6            1.15            1.5

   **10.** $3\frac{21}{100}$       3.02            1.21            3.21

| Started: | Finished: | Total Time: | Completed: | Correct: |
|----------|-----------|-------------|------------|----------|

Name _____     Date _____

**Write the decimals for the values given in questions 1–5.**

1. $\frac{6}{10}$ _____

2. $1\frac{89}{100}$ _____

3. $\frac{52}{100}$ _____

4. 22 hundredths _____

5. three and thirty-five hundredths _____

**Tom has 245 cents in his piggy bank, and Sally has $2.54 in hers.**

6. Who has more money? _____

7. What is the difference between the two amounts? _____

**Circle the value that is less in each pair.**

8. $\frac{47}{100}$    or    0.26

9. $1\frac{1}{10}$    or    1.15

10. $\frac{5}{10}$    or    0.3

| Started: | Finished: | Total Time: | Completed: | Correct: |
|---|---|---|---|---|

Name _____ Date _____

## Add the decimals.

1.  4.69
    + 2.53

2.  7.81
    + 1.52

3.  3.89
    + 2.58

4. 1.37 + 4.12 = _____

5. 1.71 + 4.18 = _____

6.  $2.75
    + $3.86

7.  $2.55
    + $6.27

8.  1.04
    3.22
    + 2.58

9.  22.16
    25.75
    + 17.15

10.  4.20
     1.20
     + 2.35

| Started: | Finished: | Total Time: | Completed: | Correct: |
|---|---|---|---|---|

Name _____     Date _____

## Subtract the decimals.

1.      4.63
      − 2.15

2.      4.77
      − 3.48

3. 2.48 − 1.46 =

4.     $8.27
      − $4.30

## Find the difference between the following measurements.

**5.** 9.65 miles and 7.50 miles _____

**6.** 6.35 feet and 3.21 feet _____

**7.** The puppy weighed 10.45 lb and the kitten weighed 6.76 lb. How much heavier was the puppy?

_____

## Find the price differences between the following menu items.

| Hamburger Combo | $7.25 |
|---|---|
| Hamburger | $3.15 |
| French Fries | $2.50 |
| Medium Drink | $1.90 |
| Apple Slices | $1.75 |

**8.** Hamburger and Medium Drink _____

**9.** French Fries and Apple Slices _____

**10.** Medium Drink and Apple Slices _____

| Started: | Finished: | Total Time: | Completed: | Correct: |
|---|---|---|---|---|

Name _____     Date _____

## Add and subtract the decimals.

1.    6.31
      + 2.38

2.    3.54
      + 4.37

3.    5.14
      + 3.67

4.    6.54
      − 1.23

5.    2.46
      − 1.91

6.    7.95
      − 2.64

## Find the sum of the following numbers. Write your answer in digits.

7. three and seventeen hundredths

   two and twenty-five hundredths

   sum = _____

8. six and twenty-two hundredths

   five and fourteen hundredths

   three and sixty-seven hundredths

   sum = _____

## Find the difference between the following numbers. Write your answer in digits.

9. seven and eighty-four hundredths

   four and sixty-five hundredths

   difference = _____

10. five and eighty-seven hundredths

    one and ninety-five hundredths

    difference = _____

| Started: | Finished: | Total Time: | Completed: | Correct: |
|---|---|---|---|---|

Name _____     Date _____

## What percentage of each hundreds square is shaded?

**1.**

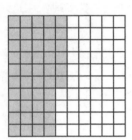

_____

**2.**

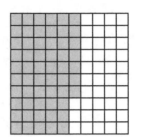

_____

## For each hundreds square, shade the given percentage.

**3.** 64%

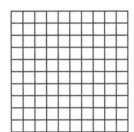

**4.** 77%

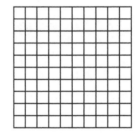

## Complete the following.

**5.** 20% means _____ out of 100.

**6.** _____ means 50 out of 100.

**7.** There were 100 students at the school and 25% were boys. How many were girls?

_____

## Write the percentage that means the following.

**8.** one-half        **9.** one-tenth        **10.** 63 out of 100

_____        _____        _____

| Started: | Finished: | Total Time: | Completed: | Correct: |
|----------|-----------|-------------|------------|----------|

Name _____    Date _____

## Circle the greater amount in each pair.

1.    20%      or      75%

2.    15%      or      10%

3.    18%      or      80%

## Complete the following table.

|     | Decimal | Fraction | Percent |
| --- | --- | --- | --- |
| 4. | 0.60 | $\frac{}{100}$ | ___% |
| 5. | 0.15 | $\frac{}{100}$ | ___% |
| 6. | 0.___ | $\frac{35}{100}$ | ___% |
| 7. | 0.___ | $\frac{7}{10}$ | ___% |
| 8. | 0.___ | $\frac{}{100}$ | 22% |
| 9. | 0.___ | $\frac{}{10}$ | 80% |

## Solve the following word problem.

10. Riley gave 10% of his 50 marbles to Jackson. How many marbles did he give?

_____

| Started: | Finished: | Total Time: | Completed: | Correct: |
| --- | --- | --- | --- | --- |

Name _____      Date _____

**Write the following fractions as decimals.**

   **1.** $\frac{1}{10}$ _____

   **2.** $\frac{1}{4}$ _____

**Write the following fractions as percentages.**

   **3.** $\frac{3}{4}$ _____

   **4.** $\frac{2}{10}$ _____

**Use <, >, or = to make the following statements true.**

   **5.** 0.99 ☐ 99%

   **6.** 5% ☐ 0.5

   **7.** 50% ☐ $\frac{1}{10}$

**There are 20 students in a class.**

   **8.** If 50% like music, how many like music?

   _____

   **9.** If 20% buy their lunch, how many buy their lunch?

   _____

   **10.** If 25% ride a bike to school, how many students ride a bike to school?

   _____

| Started: | Finished: | Total Time: | Completed: | Correct: |
|----------|-----------|-------------|------------|----------|

Name _____  Date _____

 art set
$16.75

 pencils
$5.75

 scissors
$2.15

 glue
$1.10

 highlighter
$4.39

 calculator
$25.95

**What single bill could cover the cost of the following items?**

**1.** art set _____

**2.** scissors _____

**3.** highlighter _____

**4.** pencils _____

**If you had $10, would you be able to buy the following?**

**5.** 2 highlighters? _____

**6.** an art set? _____

**7.** the glue and scissors? _____

**How many of each bill below makes $100?**

**8.** $50 _____

**9.** $20 _____

**10.** $5 _____

| Started: | Finished: | Total Time: | Completed: | Correct: |
|----------|-----------|-------------|------------|----------|

Name _____     Date _____

## Add the following amounts.

| | | | |
|---|---|---|---|
| **1.** | $3.75<br>+ $2.98 | **2.** | $4.24<br>+ $5.47 |

**3.**   $7.11<br>+ $4.53

## Subtract the following amounts.

**4.**   $6.27<br>− $2.35

**5.**   $8.25<br>− $4.21

**6.** If Alec bought 2 bags of apples at $3.60 a bag, how much change would he get back after paying with a $20 bill?

_____

**7.** Lisa is saving her money to buy a new bike helmet that costs $25.50. She has $16.36. How much more does Lisa need to save?

_____

## Find the change from $9.00, if I spent:

**8.** $5.50 _____

**9.** $2.90 _____

**10.** $4.55 _____

| Started: | Finished: | Total Time: | Completed: | Correct: |
|---|---|---|---|---|

Name _____ Date _____

**How many of each of the following bills or coins are needed to make $20?**

**1.** 50¢ _____

**2.** $1 _____

**3.** $5 _____

**Share the following amounts. How much will each person get?**

**4.** $100 among 10 teachers _____

**5.** $2 among 4 people _____

**Find the total cost of the following purchases.**

**6.** 4 bunches of flowers at $10 each _____

**7.** 10 pencils at 30¢ each _____

**How much money do you have in total if you have:**

**8.** seven $5 bills _____

**9.** three $20 bills _____

**10.** five 25¢ coins _____

| Started: | Finished: | Total Time: | Completed: | Correct: |
|---|---|---|---|---|

Name _____ Date _____

**Round each of the following amounts to the nearest 5 cents.**

**1.** 69¢ _____

**2.** 24¢ _____

**3.** 42¢ _____

**Round each of the following amounts to the nearest 10 cents.**

**4.** $0.35 _____

**5.** $1.44 _____

**Add or subtract each of the following amounts. Then round the answer to the nearest 5 cents.**

**6.**   $2.95
     + $1.73

**7.**   $5.15
     − $1.91

rounded = _____            rounded = _____

**Estimate by first rounding each of the amounts to the nearest whole dollar before adding or subtracting.**

**8.** $4.95 + $6.15 + $2.25 =

_____

**9.** $11.20 + $2.05 + $5.69 =

_____

**10.** $19.75 − $8.10 =

_____

| Started: | Finished: | Total Time: | Completed: | Correct: | |
|---|---|---|---|---|---|

Name _____ Date _____

## Complete each clock to show the time given.

| | |
|---|---|
| **1.** <br> 5 minutes to 7 | **2.** <br> 20 minutes past 3 |
| **3.** <br> half past 8 | **4.** <br> quarter past 6 |

## How many minutes does it take the minute hand to:

**5.** move from the 4 to the 5? _____

**6.** move from the 12 to the 6? _____

**7.** move from the 12 to the 11? _____

## Write the time that is one minute after the following times.

**8.** 15 minutes past 6:00 _____

**9.** 25 minutes to 7:00 _____

**10.** 10 minutes past 2:00 _____

| Started: | Finished: | Total Time: | Completed: | Correct: |
|---|---|---|---|---|

Name _____ Date _____

## Use < or > to make the statements true.

**1.** 5 days    ☐    1 week

**2.** 20 hours    ☐    1 day

**3.** 19 days    ☐    2 weeks

## Complete the label for each time shown.

| **4.** | **5.** |
|---|---|
| `4:26` | `6:49` |
| _____ minutes past _____ | _____ minutes to _____ |

## How many minutes will it take to reach the next hour?

| **6.** | **7.** |
|---|---|
| `4:44` | `7:06` |
| _____ minutes | _____ minutes |

## On each clock face, draw the time given and then write it in digital form below.

**8.** quarter past 7      **9.** half past 2      **10.** quarter to 1

| Started: | Finished: | Total Time: | Completed: | Correct: |
|---|---|---|---|---|

Name _____　Date _____

**Complete each shape so that it is symmetrical.**

1.

2.

**Which of the following are symmetrical? Write *yes* for those that are and *no* for those that are not.**

3. △ _____

4. ⬭ _____

5. G _____

6. 0 _____

**Complete the following table.**

|     | Shape | # of Sides | # of Lines of Symmetry |
|-----|-------|------------|------------------------|
| 7.  | △     |            |                        |
| 8.  | ☐     |            |                        |
| 9.  | ⬠     |            |                        |
| 10. | ⬡     |            |                        |

| Started: | Finished: | Total Time: | Completed: | Correct: |
|----------|-----------|-------------|------------|----------|

Name _____     Date _____

## Identify whether a shape is 2-dimensional (2D) or 3-dimensional (3D).

**1.** ▽ _____

**2.** _____

## Draw each of the following shapes.

| **3.** circle | **4.** hexagon | **5.** rectangle |
|---|---|---|
| | | |

## Name each of the following shapes. Use the word list in the box to help.

| star | octagon | triangle | pentagon | oval |
|---|---|---|---|---|

**6.** _____     **7.** _____

**8.** _____     **9.** _____

**10.** _____

| Started: | Finished: | Total Time: | Completed: | Correct: |
|---|---|---|---|---|

Name _____    Date _____

## Find the total number of angles in:

**1.** 4 squares _____

**2.** 3 triangles _____

**3.** 2 pentagons _____

**4.** 3 octagons _____

## Draw each of the following.

| **5.** a shape that has three angles | **6.** a shape with four equal angles and 4 equal sides |
|---|---|
| | |
| | |

## Name a real-life object that comes in the following shapes.

**7.** circle _____

**8.** octagon _____

**9.** rectangle _____

**10.** triangle _____

| Started: | Finished: | Total Time: | Completed: | Correct: |
|---|---|---|---|---|

Name _____ Date _____

## Name the following regular shapes.

1. ☐ _____

2. △ _____

3. ⬠ _____

## Name the following irregular shapes (names based on number of sides).

4. _____

5. _____

6. _____

## Draw the following shapes.

| **7.** equilateral triangle | **8.** regular pentagon |
|---|---|
| **9.** rectangle | **10.** irregular nonagon |

| Started: | Finished: | Total Time: | Completed: | Correct: |
|---|---|---|---|---|

Name _____ Date _____

## Identify each figure as a line, line segment, or ray.

1.    A            B

        line     line segment     ray

2.    C            D

        line     line segment     ray

3.    E            F

        line     line segment     ray

4.    G            H

        line     line segment     ray

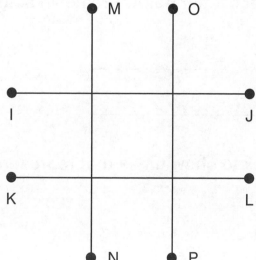

## Answer each statement.

5. $\overline{IJ}$ is parallel to _____.

6. $\overline{KL}$ intersects _____

    and _____.

7. $\overline{MN}$ is parallel to _____.

8. $\overline{OP}$ intersects _____

    and _____.

9. $\overline{OP}$ is not parallel to _____

    or _____.

10. $\overline{MN}$ does not intersect

    _____.

| Started: | Finished: | Total Time: | Completed: | Correct: |
|---|---|---|---|---|

Name _____     Date _____

**Do any of the lines in each letter below create a right (90°) angle?**
**Write *yes* or *no*.**

    **1.** T _____

    **2.** A _____

    **3.** Y _____

**Do any of the lines in each letter below create an acute (< 90°) angle?**
**Write *yes* or *no*.**

    **4.** V _____

    **5.** F _____

**Draw hands on the clock to show times that represent the following angles.**

    **6.** 90°       **7.** 180°

**Draw each of the following angles using the starting lines.**

    **8.** greater than 45°

    **9.** less than 90°

    **10.** less than 180°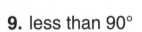

| Started: | Finished: | Total Time: | Completed: | Correct: |
|---|---|---|---|---|

Name _____ Date _____

**Use these angles to answer questions 1–7.**

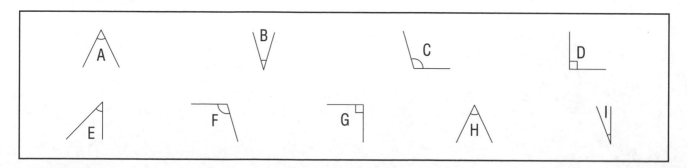

**Are the listed angles less than 90°? Write *yes* or *no*.**

    **1.** A _____

    **2.** F _____

**Find the larger angle. Circle the correct letter.**

    **3.** D or E

    **4.** B or C

    **5.** G or H

**Are the listed angles equal to 90°? Write *yes* or *no*.**

    **6.** G _____

    **7.** F _____

**Order the following angles from the smallest (1) to the largest (3).**

    **8.**  _____      **9.**  _____      **10.**  _____

| Started: | Finished: | Total Time: | Completed: | Correct: |
|---|---|---|---|---|

Name _____    Date _____

**Are the following angles acute? Write *yes* or *no*.**

1. _____

2. _____

3. _____

**Are the following angles obtuse? Write *yes* or *no*.**

4. _____

5. _____

6. _____

**Indicate whether each of the following triangles is right-angled or obtuse-angled.**

7. _____

8. _____

9. _____

10. _____

| Started: | Finished: | Total Time: | Completed: | Correct: |
|----------|-----------|-------------|------------|----------|

Name _____   Date _____

## Name each of the following solids.

1. _____

2. _____

3. _____

4. _____

## Complete the following table.

| | Solid | # of Vertices | # of Edges | # of Faces |
|---|---|---|---|---|
| 5. | | | | |
| 6. | | | | |
| 7. | | | | |
| 8. | | | | |

## What shapes do the following real-life objects best represent?

9. volcano _____

10. can of soup _____

| Started: | Finished: | Total Time: | Completed: | Correct: |
|---|---|---|---|---|

Name _____          Date _____

**Would the following nets fold to make a closed 3D shape? Write *yes* or *no*.**

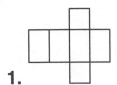                    

1. _____     2. _____     3. _____

**Name the 3D object each net will make when it is folded.**

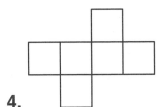          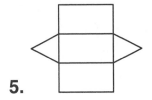          

4. _____     5. _____     6. _____

**A cross section is the face that is seen when a 3D object is cut through. For each of the following solids, draw the shape resulting from the cross section.**

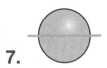     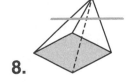     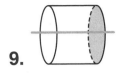     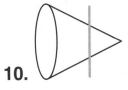

7. _____     8. _____     9. _____     10. _____

| Started: | Finished: | Total Time: | Completed: | Correct: |
|----------|-----------|-------------|------------|----------|

Name _____     Date _____

**Are these shapes quadrilaterals? Write *yes* or *no*.**

1. _____        2. _____        3. _____

**Write the number of angles inside of each of the following shapes.**

4. _____        5. _____

**Do these shapes have parallel sides? Write *yes* or *no*.**

6. _____        7. _____

**Draw each of the following.**

| 8. a triangle with three sides of different lengths | 9. a quadrilateral that has only 1 set of parallel sides |
|---|---|
| **10.** a triangle with 2 equal sides | |

| Started: | Finished: | Total Time: | Completed: | Correct: |
|---|---|---|---|---|

Name _____    Date _____

**Name the part of the circle to which the arrow is pointing—center, radius, diameter, or circumference.**

1.

_____

2.

_____

3.

_____

4.

_____

**The diameter (*d*) is twice the length of the radius (*r*). What is the diameter of each circle?**

5.

*r* = 3 in.

*d* = _____ in.

6.

*r* = 4 in.

*d* = _____ in.

7.

*r* = 2 in.

*d* = _____ in.

**The radius (*r*) is half the length of the diameter (*d*). What is the radius of each circle?**

8.

*d* = 8 in.

*r* = _____ in.

9.

*d* = 10 in.

*r* = _____ in.

10.

*d* = 6 in.

*r* = _____ in.

| Started: | Finished: | Total Time: | Completed: | Correct: |
|----------|-----------|-------------|------------|----------|

Name _____ Date _____

## Name each of the polygons.

**1.**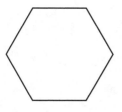

_____

**2.**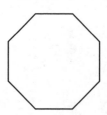

_____

**3.**

_____

**4.**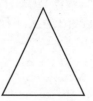

_____

## State the number of sides for the following polygons.

**5.** pentagon _____

**6.** parallelogram _____

**7.** hexagon _____

## Draw in all the lines of symmetry for each of the polygons.

**8.**

**9.**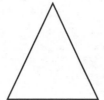

**10.**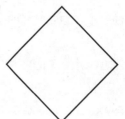

| Started: | Finished: | Total Time: | Completed: | Correct: |
| --- | --- | --- | --- | --- |

Name _____          Date _____

**Perimeter is the distance around the outside of a shape. Find the perimeter of each of the following shapes.**

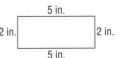

1. $P =$ _____ + _____ + _____ + _____ = _____ in.

2. $P =$ _____ + _____ + _____ = _____ in.

**A short line drawn through the sides of shapes means that those side lengths are the same. Find the perimeter of each of the following shapes.**

3.   2 in.

4.   5 cm  3 cm

5. 6 in.  8 in.

$P =$ _____

$P =$ _____

$P =$ _____

**Find the perimeter of the following rectangles.**

6. $L = 8$ cm          $W = 5$ cm          $P =$ _____

7. $L = 10$ in.          $W = 9$ in.          $P =$ _____

**Find the perimeter of the following regular shapes.**

8. pentagon, side length = 2 ft _____

9. triangle, side length = 5 in. _____

10. hexagon, side length = 6 cm _____

| Started: | Finished: | Total Time: | Completed: | Correct: |
|---|---|---|---|---|

Name _____ Date _____

**Area is the size of a surface. It is measured in square units. Find the area of the following shapes by counting the squares. Each square equals one square unit.**

**1.**

A = _____ units²

**2.**

A = _____ units²

**Find the shaded area of each shape by counting the shaded squares. Two half-shaded squares count as one shaded square.**

**3.**

A = _____ units²

**4.**

A = _____ units²

**5.**

A = _____ units²

**In squares and rectangles, area can also be found by multiplying the length by the width (A = L × W). Find the area of the following shapes.**

**6.**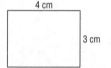

4 cm

3 cm

A = _____ cm²

**7.**

5 ft

A = _____ ft²

**8.**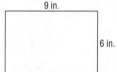

9 in.

6 in.

A = _____ in.²

**Find the area of the following triangles. First find the area as if the shape was a rectangle, then divide the area in half to find the area of the triangle, A = (L × W) ÷ 2.**

**9.**

5 cm

4 cm

A = _____ cm²

**10.**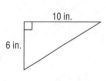

10 in.

6 in.

A = _____ in.²

| Started: | Finished: | Total Time: | Completed: | Correct: |
|----------|-----------|-------------|------------|----------|

Name _____  Date _____

## Which animal is:

**1.** left of the tiger? _____     **4.** left of the bear? _____

**2.** right of the elephant? _____     **5.** right of the tiger? _____

**3.** right of the horse? _____

**Here is a set of drawers filled with school supplies. Which item is found at each of the following positions?**

| glue | paper clips | markers |
|------|-------------|---------|
| tape | rubber bands | pencils |
| labels | staples | pens |

**6.** top left corner _____

**7.** in the center _____

**8.** right of the staples _____

**9.** far right, middle drawer _____

**10.** left of the pens _____

| Started: | Finished: | Total Time: | Completed: | Correct: |
|----------|-----------|-------------|------------|----------|

Name _____ Date _____

**Complete the compass rose using letters to represent directions.**

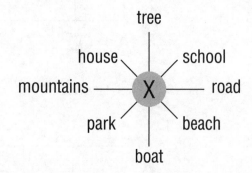

N

4._____        1._____

W        2._____

3._____        SE

S

**Tom is standing at X. What can he see if he looks:**

tree

house          school

mountains —— X —— road

park          beach

boat

**5.** south? _____

**6.** northeast? _____

**7.** west? _____

**From the X, draw:**

**8.** a star to the north.

**9.** a moon to the south.

**10.** a cloud to the northwest.

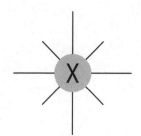

| Started: | Finished: | Total Time: | Completed: | Correct: |
|---|---|---|---|---|

Name _____ Date _____

## What shapes are found at the following coordinates?

**1.** (B, 3) _____

**2.** (C, 1) _____

**3.** (D, 3) _____

**4.** (C, 2) _____

**5.** (D, 2) _____

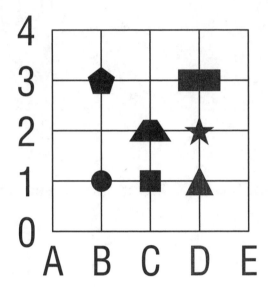

## On the grid, draw:

**6.** a diamond in (A, 2)

**7.** a rectangle in (C, 1)

**8.** a circle in (C, 4)

**9.** a triangle in (B, 3)

**10.** a star in (D, 4)

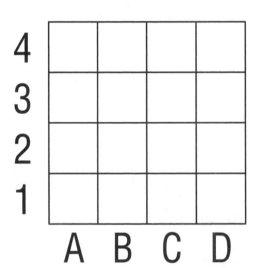

| Started: | Finished: | Total Time: | Completed: | Correct: |
|---|---|---|---|---|

Name _____ Date _____

**In a hat, there are 2 red and 2 green marbles. If Mia selects 1 marble, what is the probability she will:**

**1.** select a colored marble? _____

**2.** select a blue marble? _____

**3.** select a red marble? _____

**4.** not select a green marble? _____

**Using the words *impossible, unlikely, equal chance, likely,* and *certain,* describe the chance of landing on the shaded regions of the following spinners.**

**5.**

     _____

**6.**

     _____

**7.**

     _____

**8.**

     _____

**9.**

     _____

**10.**

     _____

| Started: | Finished: | Total Time: | Completed: | Correct: |
|---|---|---|---|---|

Name _____ Date _____

**For a class, the number of students playing each sport is shown in the graph.**

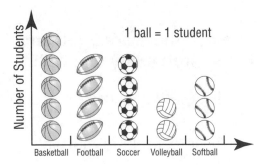

1. What was the most popular sport? _____

2. What was the least popular sport? _____

3. Which sports had equal popularity? _____

4. Which sport had three students playing? _____

5. Was football more popular than softball? _____

**Give the times during which the number of computers used was:**

| Times | Computers Used |
|-------|----------------|
| 9:00–10:00 | 🖥️🖥️ |
| 10:00–11:00 | 🖥️🖥️🖥️ |
| 11:00–12:00 | 🖥️🖥️🖥️🖥️ |
| 12:00–1:00 | 🖥️🖥️🖥️ |
| 1:00–2:00 | 🖥️🖥️🖥️🖥️🖥️ |
| 🖥️ = 5 computers ||

6. 25. _____

7. 20. _____

8. 10. _____

9. 15. _____

10. more than 15. _____

| Started: | Finished: | Total Time: | Completed: | Correct: |
|----------|-----------|-------------|------------|----------|

# Graphs and Data

Name _____  Date _____

The letters *a*, *b*, *c*, *d*, *e*, and *f* were put in a bag. One letter at a time was drawn from the bag at random and then put back. The box below shows the result of the drawings. Complete the following tally table based on these results.

| a | b | c | e | f | d | e | f | c | e |
|---|---|---|---|---|---|---|---|---|---|
| a | a | b | b | c | c | e | f | d | f |
| a | a | b | b | b | c | c | b | c | b |
| f | f | e | e | b | c | d | a | b | a |

| Letter | Tally | | Number |
|--------|-------|---|--------|
| a | 1. | | |
| b | 2. | | |
| c | 3. | | |
| d | 4. | | |
| e | 5. | | |
| f | 6. | | |

Complete the following totals of the tally table.

| Snack | Tally | Total |
|-------|-------|-------|
| fruit | ЖЖ ЖЖ II | 7. |
| chips | ЖЖ II | 8. |
| crackers | ЖЖ IIII | 9. |
| granola bars | III | 10. |

| Started: | Finished: | Total Time: | Completed: | Correct: |
|----------|-----------|-------------|------------|----------|

Name _____ Date _____

**The following bar graph shows the number of pies sold daily at the bakery for 5 days.**

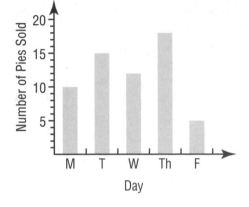

**1.** What does M stand for?

_____

**2.** How many pies were sold on Tuesday?

_____

**3.** How many pies were sold on Wednesday?

_____

**4.** What day were the least pies sold?

_____

**5.** What day were the most pies sold?

_____

**Use the tally chart to complete the bar graph.**

| Shape | Tally |
|-------|-------|
| ▲ | ⊬⊬⊦ I |
| ■ | ⊬⊬⊦ |
| ● | ⊬⊬⊦ III |
| ◆ | III |
| ★ | II |

**6.** ▲

**7.** ■

**8.** ●

**9.** ◆

**10.** ★

| Started: | Finished: | Total Time: | Completed: | Correct: |
|----------|-----------|-------------|------------|----------|

Name _____  Date _____

**For questions 1–4, using only nickels, dimes, quarters, and half-dollars, list two different ways the following amounts could be made.**

1. 25¢ _____  _____

2. 40¢ _____  _____

3. 50¢ _____  _____

4. $1.00 _____  _____

**Complete the word problems below.**

5. At the display, there were 6 spiders and 5 insects. How many legs were there all together?

_____

6. Tom spent the following amount of time doing homework for the week:  45 minutes, 30 minutes, 45 minutes, and 1 hour. How much time (in hours) did he spend doing homework all together?

_____

7. If each person at a party received $\frac{1}{4}$ of a pizza and there were 11 people, how many pizzas were there?

_____

**Find the mistake in each of the following problems. Write the correct answers.**

| 8. | 9. | 10. $5 \times 20 = 10$ |
|---|---|---|
| 426 | 671 | |
| + 318 | − 143 | |
| 734 | 538 | |

| Started: | Finished: | Total Time: | Completed: | Correct: |
|---|---|---|---|---|

Name _____  Date _____

**Reminders:**

| | |
|---|---|
| = is equal to | ≠ is not equal to |
| > is greater than | < is less than |
| ( ), ( )( ), or • mean to multiply | / means to divide |

**Complete these problems and write the answers.**

**1.** $3(9) + 4 =$ _____

**2.** $(5)(11) + 6 =$ _____

**3.** $8(6) - 6(4) =$ _____

**4.** $(20)(1)(0) =$ _____

**5.** $3(30) - 16 =$ _____

**Simplify both sides of each number statement, then rewrite each number statement using the simplified expressions.**

**6.** $\frac{6}{3} > 1 + 0$ _____

**7.** $3 + 11 < 2 + 20$ _____

**8.** $(4)(6) \neq 42$ _____

**9.** $3 \times 6 = 2 \cdot 9$ _____

**10.** $(8)(8) = 4 \times 16$ _____

| Started: | Finished: | Total Time: | Completed: | Correct: |
|---|---|---|---|---|

Name _____   Date _____

**Evaluate these expressions where n = 10.**

**1.** $n + 7 + 16 =$ _____

**2.** $9n + 7 =$ _____

**3.** $n \times 8 \times 3 =$ _____

**4.** $\dfrac{100}{n} =$ _____

**Write the missing factor that is represented by the triangle.**

**5.** $7 \times \Delta = 56$ _____

**6.** $\Delta \times 12 = 144$ _____

**7.** $\Delta \times 10 = 110$ _____

**Fill in the blank with the number that makes each number sentence true.**

**8.** $17 + 3 = 13 +$ _____

**9.** _____ $+ 7 = 11 + 2$

**10.** $32 - 8 =$ _____ $+ 11$

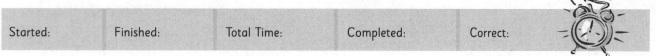

| Started: | Finished: | Total Time: | Completed: | Correct: |
|----------|-----------|-------------|------------|----------|

Name _____ Date _____

**Simplify the problems. Remember that you should always do the operations within the parentheses first.**

**1.** $(4 + 6) - 5 =$ _____

**2.** $9 + (18 - 8) =$ _____

**3.** $(15 + 15) - (16 - 15) =$ _____

**4.** $(25 - 10) + (12 - 5) =$ _____

**5.** $(18 - 9) - (20 - 13) =$ _____

**Simplify the problems. Remember that you should multiply and divide in order from left to right before you add or subtract.**

**6.** $48 \div 8 \times 6 + 4 =$ _____

**7.** $16 \div 4 + 28 \div 7 =$ _____

**8.** $9(8) + 6 \times 4 =$ _____

**9.** $7 - 4 + 2 \times 9 =$ _____

**10.** $10 \times 3 \div 6 \times 9 =$ _____

| Started: | Finished: | Total Time: | Completed: | Correct: |
|---|---|---|---|---|

Name _____  Date _____

**In these magic squares, numbers are arranged so that they add up to the same total vertically, horizontally, and diagonally. Complete each magic square for the total given.**

**1.** 15:

| 8 |   | 6 |
|---|---|---|
|   |   | 7 |
|   | 9 |   |

**2.** 27:

| 15 |    |    |
|----|----|----|
|    |    | 13 |
| 7  | 17 |    |

**Work backwards to find the original number, if I started with that number and:**

**3.** x 2, then + 5, and the solution was 15. _____

**4.** ÷ 3, then − 8, and the solution was 1. _____

**For the tangram, name each of the labeled shapes.**

**5.** _____

**6.** _____

**7.** _____

**8.** _____

**9.** _____

**10.** _____

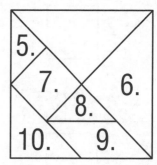

| Started: | Finished: | Total Time: | Completed: | Correct: |
|----------|-----------|-------------|------------|----------|

Name _____  Date _____

**Write the missing number for each problem. Each number can be used only one time.**

| 51 | 52 | 53 | 54 | 55 | 56 | 57 | 58 | 59 | 60 |

1.   5   x   12   =   ☐

2.   4   x   13   =   ☐

3.   61   –   ☐   =   2

4.   28   +   28   =   ☐

5.   ☐   ÷   11   =   5

6.   9   x   6   =   ☐

7.   ☐   ÷   3   =   17

8.   39   +   ☐   =   92

9.   ☐   –   23   =   34

10.   29   x   2   =   ☐

Pages in *Timed Math Practice* meet one or more of the following Common Core State Standards.

© Copyright 2010. National Governors Association Center for Best Practices and Council of Chief State School Officers. All rights reserved. For more information about the Common Core State Standards, go to **http://www.corestandards.org**

| Mathematics Standards | Test |
|---|---|
| **Operations and Algebraic Thinking** | |
| Use the four operations with whole numbers to solve problems. | 7, 9, 13, 14, 15, 16, 17, 18, 19, 20, 21, 22, 23, 24, 25, 26, 27, 28, 29, 30, 31, 32, 33, 34, 37, 38, 39, 40, 41, 42, 43, 44, 45, 46, 47, 96, 97, 98, 99, 100 |
| Gain familiarity with factors and multiples. | 8, 29, 35, 36 |
| Generate and analyze patterns. | 5, 11, 12, 48, 58 |
| **Number and Operations in Base Ten** | |
| Generalize place value understanding for multi-digit whole numbers. | 1, 2, 3, 4, 5, 6, 10, 56, 57, 58 |
| **Number and Operations—Fractions** | |
| Extend understanding of fraction equivalence and ordering. | 49, 50, 51, 52, 53, 54 |
| Build fractions from unit fractions by applying and extending previous understandings of operations on whole numbers. | 95 |
| Understand decimal notation for fractions, and compare decimal fractions. | 54, 55, 56, 59, 60, 63, 65, 66 |
| **Measurement and Data** | |
| Solve problems involving measurement and conversion of measurements from a larger unit to a smaller unit. | 61, 62, 67, 68, 69, 70, 71, 72, 86, 87, 95 |
| **Geometry** | |
| Draw and identify lines and angles, and classify shapes by properties of their lines and angles. | 73, 74, 75, 76, 77, 78, 79, 80, 81, 83, 84, 85, 99 |

# Answer Key

## Test 1—Page 5
1. 4,364
2. 5,340
3. 5,007
4. 7,372
5. 5,011
6. 2,101
7. 2,021
8. one thousand, two hundred seventy-five
9. two thousand, forty-one
10. seven thousand, nine

## Test 2—Page 6
1. 2,184
2. 9,026
3. 6,361
4. six thousand, four hundred twenty
5. seven thousand, three hundred sixty-eight
6. four thousand, sixty-seven
7. three thousand, four hundred eighty-five

| | Thousands | Hundreds | Tens | Ones |
|---|---|---|---|---|
| 8. | 3 | 1 | 1 | 1 |
| 9. | 2 | 3 | 6 | 1 |
| 10. | 9 | 4 | 2 | 6 |

## Test 3—Page 7
1. 300
2. 80
3. 5
4. 8,000
5. false
6. true
7. true
8. 874
9. 3,478
10. 8,743

## Test 4—Page 8
1. 2,011; 2,065; 2,089; 2,111
2. 3,003; 3,033; 3,303; 3,330
3. 1,824; 2,649; 3,841; 8,916
4. 8,970; 7,860; 6,980; 6,650
5. 1,111; 1,101; 1,011; 1,010
6. 5,905; 5,609; 5,403; 5,302
7. 1,369; 1,379; 1,389; 1,399; 1,409
8. 8,008; 8,010
9. 4,025; 4,030
10. 3,070; 3,060

## Test 5—Page 9
1. 2,000
2. 8,000
3. 7,000
4. 5,249
5. 9,456
6. 4,346
7. 6,052
8. 6,111;  7,111
9. 3,789;  2,789
10. 4,006;  3,006

## Test 6—Page 10
1. 7,631
2. 1,904
3. 3,333
4. 5,000 + 500 + 20 + 8
5. 2,000 + 900+ 90 +9
6. 6,000 + 700 + 9
7. 7,000 + 100 + 1
8.  8  8  7  6
9.  4  2  0  1
10.  6  3  6  9

## Test 7—Page 11
1. 1st
2. 8th
3. 6th
4. 12th
5. 21st
6. 12th, 13th, 14th, 15th, 16th
7. 96th, 97th, 98th, 99th, 100th
8. 3rd
9. 5th
10. 50th

## Test 8—Page 12
1. 1, 7
2. 1, 23
3. 1, 2, 3, 4, 6, 12
4. false
5. true
6. false
7. true
8. prime
9. composite
10. composite

## Test 9—Page 13
1. double 10 = 20
   double 20 = 40
   $4 \times 10 = 40$
2. double 15 = 30
   double 30 = 60
   $4 \times 15 = 60$
3. double 21 = 42
   double 42 = 84
   $4 \times 21 = 84$
4. 25
5. 3,000
6. 7,500
7. 64 legs
8. 100 legs
9. 200 legs
10. 160 legs

## Test 10—Page 14
1. 1,020
2. 3,704
3. 999
4. 3,752
5. false
6. false
7. true
8. <
9. <
10. >

## Test 11—Page 15
1. 103, 106, 109, 112, 115
2. 95, 90, 85, 80, 75
3. 246, 236, 226, 216, 206
4. 3,516; 3,616; 3,716; 3,816; 3,916
5. add 50
6. subtract 7
7. subtract 100
8. 40, 56
9. 581, 573
10. 40, 80

## Test 12—Page 16
1. 28, 33, 38, 43, 48, 53
   The rule is:  add 5
2. 17, 15, 13, 11, 9, 7
   The rule is:  subtract 2
3. 85, 97, 109, 121, 133, 145
   The rule is:  add 12
4. 43, 50, 57, 64, 71, 78
   The rule is:  add 7
5. 99, 109, 119, 129, 139, 149
   The rule is:  add 10
6. The rule is:  multiply by 2
7. The rule is:  multiply by 5
8. The rule is:  divide by 3
9. The rule is:  divide by 2
10. The rule is:  multiply by 10

## Test 13—Page 17

1. 77
2. 94
3. 99
4. 95
5. 39 horses
6. 38
7. 68
8. 21 + 22
9. 41 + 15
10. 36 + 53

## Test 14—Page 18

1. 937
2. 995
3. 596
4. 170
5. 398
6. 999
7. 642 cards
8. 90,  87
9. 80,  79
10. 100,  96

## Test 15—Page 19

1. 4,699
2. 8,888
3. 7,899
4. 8,478
5. 9,895
6. 5,676
7. 4,788 paper clips
8. 3,694
9. 7,543
10. 1,278

## Test 16—Page 20

1. 861
2. 806
3. 828
4. 664
5. 900
6. 631
7. 586 pens and pencils
8. erasers and pencils
9. crayons and pencils
10. crayons, erasers, and pencils

## Test 17—Page 21

1. 5,046
2. 7,308
3. 9,794
4. 7,980
5. 4,872 newspapers
6. 1,360 fish
7. 5,685 lemons
8. 5,740; 4,259
9. 8,137; 1,862
10. 5,000; 4,999

## Test 18—Page 22

1. 6,921
2. 7,650
3. 3,754
4. $9,175
5. $6,622
6. $6,044
7. $8,000
8. 734
9. 2,969
10. 8,350

## Test 19—Page 23

1. 31
2. 26
3. 32
4. 54
5. 32 sheep
6. 41 cards
7. 11 chocolates
8. 21 bunches
9. 34 bunches
10. 12 bunches

## Test 20—Page 24

1. 37
2. 17
3. 34
4. false
5. false
6. true
7. 25
8. $47
9. $13
10. $54

## Test 21—Page 25

1. 822
2. 631
3. 123
4. 174
5. 481
6. 133
7. 120
8. $133
9. $210
10. $41

## Test 22—Page 26

1. 326
2. 406
3. 491
4. 45
5. 81, 81, 142
6. 246, 246, 475
7. 479, 479, 800
8. 117 more cows
9. 272 more sheep
10. 389 more cows

## Test 23—Page 27

1. 1,522
2. 1,135
3. 2,240
4. 2,346
5. 4,627
   $$\begin{array}{r} -\,2{,}316 \\ \hline 2{,}311 \end{array}$$
6. 7,493
   $$\begin{array}{r} -\,6{,}243 \\ \hline 1{,}250 \end{array}$$
7. $$\begin{array}{r} 5{,}776 \\ -\,2{,}415 \\ \hline 3{,}361 \end{array}$$
8. 6,431
9. 1,346
10. 5,085

## Test 24—Page 28

1. 3,080
2. 1,153
3. 1,549
4. 3,478
5. 2,685
6. 2,204
7. 4,586
8. 2,549
9. 3,015
10. 1,375

## Test 25—Page 29

1. 700
2. 1,000
3. 8,000
4. 150
5. 280
6. 5,600
7. 8,400
8. 4,965; 4,835
9. 4,775
10. 4,665; 4,595

## Test 26—Page 30

1. 30 + 50 = 80
2. 410 + 90 = 500
3. 140 − 40 = 100
4. 50 + 100 + 200 = 350
5. 100 − 30 − 10 − 10 = 50
6. 500 − 180 − 60 − 60 = 200
7. 130 + 130 + 130 + 130 = 520
8. 160      161      1
9. 380      375      5
10. 280      274      6

## Test 27—Page 31

1. 12
2. 6, 24
3. 5, 15
4. 48, 48
5. 32, 32, 64, 64
6. 56, 56, 112, 112
7. 66, 66, 132, 132
8. 80 + 32, 112
9. 60 + 18, 78
10. 50 + 40, 90

# Answer Key (cont.)

## Test 28—Page 32
1. 8, 4, 2, 1
2. 80, 40, 20, 10, 5
3. 128, 64, 32, 16, 8, 4, 2, 1
4. 18, 36, 72, 144, 288
5. 10, 20, 40, 80, 160
6. 200; 400; 800; 1,600; 3,200
7. answer should be 566
8. answer should be 239
9. true
10. false

## Test 29—Page 33
1. 24
2. 22
3. 36
4. 20
5. 56
6. 4, 8, 12, 16, 20, 24, 28, 32, 36, 40
7. 64 wheels
8. 72 legs
9. 32 legs
10. 24 legs

## Test 30—Page 34
1. 60
2. 30
3. 0
4. 45
5. 110
6. true
7. true
8. 5  40  10  35  15  30  20  25
9. 45  0  50  25  55  35  60  15
10. 0  70  10  60  20  50  30  40

## Test 31—Page 35
1. 72
2. 30
3. 42
4. 4, 2
5. 6, 36
6. 3, 6
7. $30
8. $7 \times 3 = 21$
9. $6 \times 2 = 12$
10. $11 \times 3 = 33$

## Test 32—Page 36
1. 35
2. 48
3. 72
4. false
5. true
6. false
7. 58, 66, 74, 82, 90, 98, 106, 114, 122, 130
8. 0  28  7  35  14  42  21  49
9. 48  16  40  24  32  0  56  8
10. 27  99  72  90  36  81  9  108

## Test 33—Page 37
1. 80
2. 63
3. 40
4. $48
5. $14
6. 30, 5
7. 2, 18
8. 48  56  64  72
9. 45  54  63  72
10. 40  45  50  55

## Test 34—Page 38
1. 4
2. 49
3. 81
4. 15
5. 21
6. 6
7. 10
8. 9 dots drawn
9. 16 dots drawn
10. 25 dots drawn

## Test 35—Page 39
1. true
2. false
3. true
4. Possible answers: 1, 2, 3, 4, 6, 12
5. Possible answers: 1, 5, 7, 35
6. Possible answers: 1, 2, 4, 8, 16, 32
7. 15
8. 10, 12, 18
9. 12, 18, 21
10. 21

## Test 36—Page 40
1. 1, 5
2. 1, 11
3. 1, 23
4. false
5. true
6. 1, 15, 3, 5,
7. 1, 24, 2, 12, 3, 8, 4, 6
8. 1, 36, 2, 18, 3, 12, 4, 9, 6
9. 1, 18, 2, 9, 3, 6
10. Circle 1, 2, 3, 6, 9, 18

## Test 37—Page 41
1. 50 + 30, 80
2. 60 + 54, 114
3. $4 \times 8$, 80 + 32, 112
4. 200
5. 480
6. 320
7. 3,200
8. 3,000
9. 2,700
10. 2,800

## Test 38—Page 42
1. 60
2. 140
3. 560
4. 360
5. 420
6. 330
7. 810 seats
8. 300
9. 210
10. 450

## Test 39—Page 43
1. 12; 120; 1,200
2. 35; 350; 3,500
3. 128
4. 318
5. 205
6. 390
7. 208 bananas
8. 80 + 6, 86
9. $(6 \times 10) + (6 \times 6)$, 60 + 36, 96
10. $(4 \times 50) + (4 \times 3)$, 200 + 12, 212

## Test 40—Page 44
1. 9, 8
2. 7, 6
3. 12, 4
4. 9
5. 34
6. 12
7. 6 groups
8. 7 baskets
9. 5 baskets
10. 3 baskets

## Test 41—Page 45
1. 4
2. 10
3. 8
4. 3
5. 25
6. 9
7. 24
8. 8
9. 8
10. 6

**Test 42—Page 46**
1. 3
2. 8
3. 10
4. 4
5. 2
6. 9
7. 7 necklaces
8. 5 bottles in each row, 2 left over
9. 6 herds, 3 cows left over
10. 10 marbles in each group, 6 left over

**Test 43—Page 47**
1. 5 r 3
2. 8 r 2
3. 6 r 5
4. 18
5. 11 r 1
6. 6 r 3
7. 4 each with 5 left over
8. 10, 30, 6, 18
9. 8, 16, 4, 40
10. 5, 50, 100, 10

**Test 44—Page 48**
1. 24
2. 240
3. =
4. <
5. >
6. 24 eggs
7. $9.00
8. 46
9. 7
10. 20

**Test 45—Page 49**
1. 7
2. 2
3. 17
4. 27
5. 13
6. 48 chickens
7. 14 nails
8. $5 \times 7 = 35$ or $7 \times 5 = 35$
   $35 \div 7 = 5$ or $35 \div 5 = 7$
9. $3 \times 10 = 30$ or $10 \times 3 = 30$
   $30 \div 10 = 3$ or $30 \div 3 = 10$
10. $4 \times 1 = 4$ or $1 \times 4 = 4$
    $4 \div 1 = 4$ or $4 \div 4 = 1$

**Test 46—Page 50**
1. $17 + 26 = 43$, true
2. $58 + 27 = 85$, true
3. $74 + 26 \neq 90$, false
4. $60 - 21 \neq 49$ or $60 - 49 \neq 21$, false
5. $52 - 16 = 36$ or $52 - 36 = 16$, true
6. $101 - 27 \neq 84$ or $101 - 84 \neq 27$, false
7. $37 - 23 = 14$ bracelets
8. answer should be 98
9. answer should be 44
10. answer should be 14

**Test 47—Page 51**
1. 128
2. 128
3. 114
4. 107
5. 114
6. 30
7. 4
8. 20
9. 5
10. 5

**Test 48—Page 52**
1. 25, 30, 35
2. 10, 20, 40
3. 91, 82, 73
4. 125
5. 43
6. 32
7. 94
8. 13, 40, 121
9. 45, 445, 4,445
10. 18, 22, 26

**Test 49—Page 53**
1. 3/4
2. 3/8
3. 7/10
4. false
5. true
6. one-fourth
7. two-fifths
8. 3/5
9. 4/10
10. 4/8

**Test 50—Page 54**
1. 1/8, 2/8, 5/8, 7/8
2. 1/5, 2/5, 3/5, 4/5
3. 1/10, 2/10, 3/10, 4/10
4. 9/10, 8/10, 6/10, 4/10
5. 4/4, 3/4, 2/4, 1/4
6. 1/2, 4/10, 1/5, 1/10
7. 7 stars shaded
8. 1 triangle shaded
9. 1 triangle shaded
10. 5 squares shaded

**Test 51—Page 55**
1. 1/4
2. 3/4
3. 3/5
4. true
5. false
6. true
7. 5/8, 4/8, 3/8, 1/8
8. 9/10, 6/10, 3/10, 2/10
9. 1/4, 1/2, 3/4, 1
10. 5/8, 6/8, 7/8, 1

**Test 52—Page 56**
1. $\frac{1}{2} = \frac{\boxed{2}}{4}$
2. $\frac{1}{2} = \frac{\boxed{5}}{10}$
3. $\frac{3}{4} = \frac{\boxed{6}}{8}$
4. false
5. true
6. 2
7. 3
8. 10
9. 2
10. 2

**Test 53—Page 57**
1. 1 1/2
2. 2 1/4
3. 3 3/4
4. 1 1/2, 2 1/2
5. 1 1/4, 1 1/2 (or 1 2/4)
6. 1 3/5
7. 2 3/4
8. $1\frac{3}{5}$
9. $1\frac{5}{8}$
10. $1\frac{6}{8}$

**Test 54—Page 58**
1. 45/100
2. 51/100
3. 33/100
4. 290 cents
5. 175 cents
6. 505 cents
7. 0.05
8. 0.62
9. 0.40
10. 0.19

**Test 55—Page 59**
1. 0.6
2. 0.7
3. 1 1/10—1.1
4. 5/10—0.5
5. 2/10—0.2
6. 10/10—1
7. 1 7/10—1.7
8. 3/10—0.3
9. 0.7
10. 0.3

## Test 56—Page 60
1. 0.56
2. 0.30
3. 0.14
4. 5 tenths
5. 5 hundredths
6. 5 tens
7. 5 ones
8. forty-six hundredths
9. five hundredths
10. thirty hundredths or three tenths

## Test 57—Page 61
1. 0.75
2. 0.93
3. 0.40
4. 0.17
5. 0.57
6. 0.42
7. 4 tenths

| | H | T | O | . | Tths | Hths |
|---|---|---|---|---|---|---|
| 8. | 0 | 1 | 2 | . | 4 | 0 |
| 9. | 2 | 0 | 5 | . | 6 | 6 |
| 10. | 3 | 1 | 0 | . | 9 | 5 |

## Test 58—Page 62
1. 0.13
2. 0.79
3. 0.05
4. 2
5. 7
6. 4.2
7. 4.6
8. 0.05, 0.15, 0.45, 0.50
9. 1.21, 1.23, 1.27, 1.28
10. 1.46, 1.79, 2.38, 3.66

## Test 59—Page 63
1. 1.27
2. 5.06
3. 1.19
4. 1
5. 3
6. 3
7. 14.32, 17.62, 19.63, 20.58
8. 1.16
9. 1.5
10. 3.21

## Test 60—Page 64
1. 0.6
2. 1.89
3. 0.52
4. 0.22
5. 3.35
6. Sally
7. $0.09 or 9 cents
8. 0.26
9. 1 1/10
10. 0.3

## Test 61—Page 65
1. 7.22
2. 9.33
3. 6.47
4. 5.49
5. 5.89
6. $6.61
7. $8.82
8. 6.84
9. 65.06
10. 7.75

## Test 62—Page 66
1. 2.48
2. 1.29
3. 1.02
4. $3.97
5. 2.15 mi.
6. 3.14 ft.
7. 3.69 lb.
8. $1.25
9. $0.75
10. $0.15

## Test 63—Page 67
1. 8.69
2. 7.91
3. 8.81
4. 5.31
5. 0.55
6. 5.31
7. 5.42
8. 15.03
9. 3.19
10. 3.92

## Test 64—Page 68
1. 46%
2. 57%
3.
4.
5. 20
6. 50%
7. 75 were girls
8. 50%
9. 10%
10. 63%

## Test 65—Page 69
1. 75%
2. 15%
3. 80%

| | Decimal | Fraction | Percent |
|---|---|---|---|
| 4. | 0.60 | 60/100 | 60% |
| 5. | 0.15 | 15/100 | 15% |
| 6. | 0.35 | 35/100 | 35% |
| 7. | 0.70 or 0.7 | 7/10 | 70% |
| 8. | 0.22 | 22/100 | 22% |
| 9. | 0.80 or 0.8 | 8/10 | 80% |

10. 5

## Test 66—Page 70
1. 0.10
2. 0.25
3. 75%
4. 20%
5. =
6. <
7. >
8. 10 like music
9. 4 buy lunch
10. 5 ride a bike

## Test 67—Page 71
1. $20
2. $5
3. $5
4. $10
5. yes
6. no
7. yes
8. 2
9. 5
10. 20

## Test 68—Page 72
1. $6.73
2. $9.71
3. $11.64
4. $3.92
5. $4.04
6. $12.80
7. $9.14
8. $3.50
9. $6.10
10. $4.45

## Test 69—Page 73
1. 40
2. 20
3. 4
4. $10
5. 50¢
6. $40
7. $3
8. $35
9. $60
10. $1.25

## Test 70—Page 74
1. 70¢
2. 25¢
3. 40¢
4. $0.40
5. $1.40
6. $4.68, $4.70
7. $3.24, $3.25
8. $5 + $6 + $2 = $13
9. $11 + $2 + $6 = $19
10. $20 − $8 = $12

# Answer Key (cont.)

## Test 71—Page 75

1. 2. 3. 4.

5. 5 min
6. 30 min
7. 55 min
8. 6:16
9. 6:36
10. 2:11

## Test 72—Page 76

1. <
2. <
3. >
4. 26 minutes past 4
5. 11 minutes to 7
6. 16 minutes
7. 54 minutes

8. 9. 10.

7:15  2:30  12:45

## Test 73—Page 77

1. ⊘  2. ☆

3. yes
4. no
5. no

6. yes
7. 3, 3
8. 4, 4
9. 5, 5
10. 6, 6

## Test 74—Page 78

1. 2D
2. 3D
3. ○
4. ⬡
5. ▭

6. triangle
7. pentagon
8. oval
9. star
10. octagon

## Test 75—Page 79

1. 16
2. 9
3. 10
4. 24
5. check drawing (triangle)

6. check drawing (square)
7. answers will vary
8. answers will vary
9. answers will vary
10. answers will vary

## Test 76—Page 80

1. square
2. triangle
3. pentagon
4. pentagon
5. trapezoid

6. hexagon
7. check drawing
8. check drawing
9. check drawing
10. check drawing

## Test 77—Page 81

1. line
2. line segment
3. ray
4. line
5. $\overline{KL}$ or $\overline{LK}$

6. $\overline{MN}$ or $\overline{NM}$ and $\overline{OP}$ or $\overline{PO}$
7. $\overline{OP}$ or $\overline{PO}$
8. $\overline{IJ}$ or $\overline{JI}$ and $\overline{KL}$ or $\overline{LK}$
9. $\overline{IJ}$ or $\overline{JI}$ or $\overline{KL}$ or $\overline{LK}$
10. $\overline{OP}$ or $\overline{PO}$

## Test 78—Page 82

1. yes
2. no
3. no
4. yes
5. no

6. check drawing
7. check drawing
8. check drawing
9. check drawing
10. check drawing

## Test 79—Page 83

1. yes
2. no
3. D
4. C
5. G

6. yes
7. no
8. 1
9. 2
10. 3

## Test 80—Page 84

1. no
2. yes
3. yes
4. yes
5. yes

6. no
7. obtuse-angled
8. right-angled
9. right-angled
10. obtuse-angled

## Test 81—Page 85

1. cube
2. sphere
3. cone
4. cylinder
5. 8; 12; 6

6. 5; 8; 5
7. 4; 6; 4
8. 8; 12; 6
9. cone
10. cylinder

## Test 82—Page 86

1. yes
2. yes
3. no
4. cube
5. triangular prism
6. triangular pyramid

7. ○
8. ▢
9. ▭
10. ○

## Test 83—Page 87

1. yes
2. yes
3. yes
4. 4
5. 3

6. yes
7. no
8. check drawing (trapezoid)
9. check drawing
10. check drawing

## Test 84—Page 88

1. radius
2. center
3. diameter
4. circumference
5. 6 in.

6. 8 in.
7. 4 in.
8. 4 in.
9. 5 in.
10. 3 in.

## Test 85—Page 89

1. hexagon
2. octagon
3. trapezoid
4. triangle
5. 5
6. 4
7. 6

8. 9. 10.

## Test 86—Page 90

1. $P = 2 + 5 + 2 + 5 = 14$ in.
2. $P = 4 + 5 + 3 = 12$ in.
3. $P = 12$ in.
4. $P = 16$ cm
5. $P = 32$ in.

6. $P = 26$ cm
7. $P = 38$ cm
8. $P = 10$ ft
9. $P = 15$ in.
10. $P = 36$ cm

## Test 87—Page 91

1. 7 units$^2$
2. 6 units$^2$
3. 7 units$^2$
4. 14 units$^2$
5. 12 units$^2$

6. 12 cm$^2$
7. 25 ft$^2$
8. 54 in.$^2$
9. 10 cm$^2$
10. 30 in.$^2$

## Test 88—Page 92

1. lion
2. hippo
3. elephant
4. tiger
5. bear
6. glue
7. rubber bands
8. pens
9. pencils
10. staples

## Test 89—Page 93

1. NE
2. E
3. SW
4. NW
5. boat
6. school
7. mountains
8. check drawing
9. check drawing
10. check drawing

## Test 90—Page 94

1. pentagon
2. square
3. rectangle
4. trapezoid
5. star

6.–10.

## Test 91—Page 95

1. 4/4 or 1
2. 0
3. 2/4 or 1/2
4. 2/4 or 1/2
5. unlikely
6. certain
7. equal chance
8. equal chance
9. likely
10. impossible

## Test 92—Page 96

1. Basketball
2. Volleyball
3. Football and Soccer
4. Softball
5. yes
6. 1:00–2:00
7. 11:00–12:00
8. 9:00–10:00
9. 10:00–11:00 and 12:00–1:00
10. 11:00–12:00 and 1:00–2:00

## Test 93—Page 97

1. ⅢⅢ II, 7
2. ⅢⅢ ⅢⅢ, 10
3. ⅢⅢ III, 8
4. III, 3
5. ⅢⅢ I, 6
6. ⅢⅢ I, 6
7. 12
8. 7
9. 9
10. 3

## Test 94—Page 98

1. Monday
2. 15
3. 12
4. Friday
5. Thursday

6. ▲
7. ■
8. ●
9. ◆
10. ★

## Test 95—Page 99

1. answers will vary
2. answers will vary
3. answers will vary
4. answers will vary
5. 78 legs
6. 3 hours
7. 3 pizzas
8. answer = 744
9. answer = 528
10. answer = 100

## Test 96—Page 100

1. 31
2. 61
3. 24
4. 0
5. 74
6. 2 > 1
7. 14 < 22
8. 24 ≠ 42
9. 18 = 18
10. 64 = 64

## Test 97—Page 101

1. 33
2. 97
3. 240
4. 10
5. 8
6. 12
7. 11
8. 7
9. 6
10. 13

## Test 98—Page 102

1. 5
2. 19
3. 29
4. 22
5. 2
6. 40
7. 8
8. 96
9. 21
10. 45

## Test 99—Page 103

1. 15:

| 8 | 1 | 6 |
|---|---|---|
| 3 | 5 | 7 |
| 4 | 9 | 2 |

2. 27:

| 15 | 1 | 11 |
|----|---|----|
| 5 | 9 | 13 |
| 7 | 17 | 3 |

3. 5
4. 27
5. triangle
6. triangle
7. square
8. triangle
9. parallelogram
10. triangle

## Test 100—Page 104

1. 60
2. 52
3. 59
4. 56
5. 55
6. 54
7. 51
8. 53
9. 57
10. 58